OF *the first edition of* THE ENIGMA OF STONEHENGE
*one hundred copies have been specially
bound, numbered and signed by the author
and the artist, each with an original
photograph laid in.*

This is number   30 *of* 100.

John Fowles

JOHN FOWLES

BARRY BRUKOFF

THE ENIGMA OF STONEHENGE

This Stonage did astonish them, and did amaze
them, that they durst not labour, lest they should
lose their labour, and themselves also. And if the
grand Seniors, which lived so near it, above a
thousand years since, could not, how shall we sillie
freshmen unlock this Closet?

A Fool's Bolt Soon Shott at Stonage

JONATHAN CAPE
THIRTY BEDFORD SQUARE
LONDON

THE ENIGMA OF
STONEHENGE

John Fowles & Barry Brukoff

To my son, Christopher David Brukoff B.B.

First published 1980
Text © 1980 by The Philpot Museum
Photographs © 1980 by Barry Brukoff

Jonathan Cape Limited, 30 Bedford Square, London WC1

All rights, title and interest in the works of Barry Brukoff
are the property of Barry Brukoff. Prints of his photographs
may be purchased from him at 1620 Montgomery Street, San Francisco,
California 94111. Phone (415) 781–8736

British Library Cataloguing in Publication Data
Brukoff, Barry
    The enigma of stonehenge.
    1. Stonehenge
    I. Title II. Fowles, John
    936.2'3'19   DA142

ISBN 0–224–01618–0

Printed in Italy by Arnoldo Mondadori Editore, Verona

THE PRESENT

MY EARLIEST MEMORY of Stonehenge is, like so many childhood memories, as much fiction as fact. I see a little boy standing at a country roadside. Larks sing, lapwings wheel. There across the cropped greensward the great stones rise and I run towards them, ahead of my parents – not at all, I'm afraid, as a budding scholar or an embryo Romantic. But at least I recognize a good natural exploring place when I see one. Climbing, scrambling, squeezing through stone pillars: it is not quite so jolly as Cheddar Gorge or the Valley of the Rocks, but above all it is not suburban, the world I know best. Already I know suburbia is sameness, sameness, sameness; that freedom, or my freedom, lies in the unsame; and that nothing can be unsamer than this.

One part of my memory must be very wrong, because people have not been allowed to walk up to the monument as they like since well before my birth; and even in the 1930s I am pretty sure, though one was then free to wander in the central circle, that eight-year-old mountaineers were not encouraged. But our present protectiveness and seriousness over the place is something new. Even possessing it, as late as 1915, had a remarkable casualness. A gentleman bought it at auction for £6,600 in that year. He was asked why. It emerged that his wife had happened to mention at breakfast that 'she would like to own it'. The good man promptly sallied out and bought her her stone necklace. (She did not wear it long, however; three years later the Chubbs generously gave ownership to the nation.)

Of one thing I am certain: my own first meeting was happy. It may have been because I could not quite take that enticing clutter of boulders, so like a Dartmoor hilltop, as man-made, whatever I had been told beforehand. Almost all public buildings have always carried strong connotations in my mind of duty, work, imprisonment of one form or another – of the cell in all its senses. Where the wiser judge architecture by the way it plays with light and space, I tend to judge it by what it shuts out of those things. Stonehenge's marvellous openness to them was what first pleased me. It came to me on that occasion, and has remained since, as the most natural building, the most woven with light, sky and space, in the world.

My latest remembrance, on a recent clear but arctic November day, is sadly different. Stonehenge stands in the fork of two busy roads, and the dominant sound in its present landscape is not the larksong of my memory, but the rather less poetic territorial whine of the long-distance truck. Visitors get to it now from a car-park, past a sunken 'sales complex', then down a subway under the nearest road: all this designed not to spoil the view, but the effect is unhappily reminiscent of an underground bunker. When they finally rise inside the wired-off enclosure, they are promptly faced with another barrier. The public is now forbidden the central area.

Conservation is a fine thing; yet one feels in some way cheated of a birthright, while the stone-grove itself seems deprived of an essential scale – indeed rather like a group of frightened aboriginals huddled together in self-defence against this sudden decision on our part to ostracize them so mercilessly. Everyone I had spoken to before coming had warned me that the new preserved-for-posterity Stonehenge – this was my first experience of it – makes a depressing visit. My wife, more fastidious than I am, took one look and turned back to the car.

I went up to an attendant in a little wind-shelter and explained I was preparing a text to accompany Barry Brukoff's photographs and would like to walk inside the barrier.

'Are you an archaeologist?'

'No. Just a writer.'

'Department of the Environment, London. By letter.' Then he added, 'And I can tell you now you'll be wasting your time.'

He looked bleakly over my shoulder at the mute clump of stones, as a prison warder might who has successfully foiled yet another clumsy escape attempt. I didn't really blame him, for it was bitterly cold; and after all, who cares for mere curiosity and affection any more?

We didn't stop long later that day at Avebury, which lies some twenty miles' drive north of Stonehenge – and the last of them very beautiful miles, if one takes the old by-road up through Woodborough, across Wansdyke and the Ridgeway. Nothing, thank goodness, can destroy the ancient majesty of the Avebury circles and stone-rows: and I had come simply to get the taste of contemporary Stonehenge out of my mouth. We stayed the night at Marlborough, then early next morning parked at a roadside just before Silbury Hill and walked up a mile of frost-rimed fields to one of the least visited and least spoilt of the great Wiltshire Neolithic monuments, the long barrow at West Kennet; and there before its entrance colonnade of megaliths, standing eternally on guard like a line of very ancient soldiers, or totem-poles – the latter not so far-fetched a simile as it may sound, as I shall explain – I began to regain my good temper and affection for this most haunted of southern English landscapes.

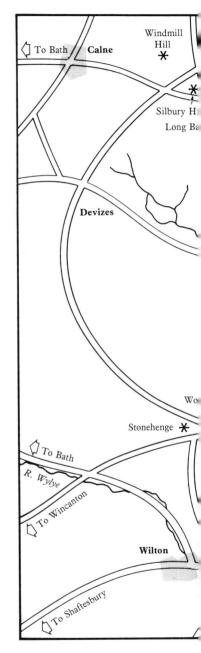

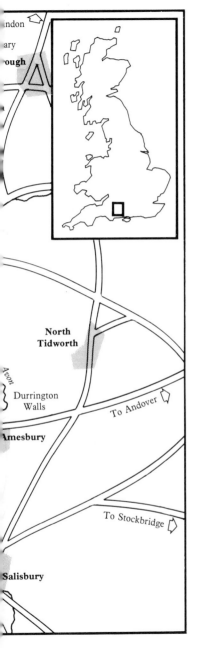

The world has greater memorials to the dead than West Kennet, and more celebrated ones, but very, very few of such massive simplicity and dignity – or age, for it is the earliest example of local prehistoric man's skill at handling huge weights, whose apotheosis is Stonehenge. It stands quite alone, on a ridge facing the largest ancient man-made object in Europe, the strange 'pyramid' of Silbury. The little cells inside the barrow have long been bereft of their bones by the archaeologists, yet death still lingers in their air – but it is not death the horror, the dread marauding skeleton on horseback. Here one feels a very long, quiet peace, almost a domesticity, a sleeping stone womb.

This day the arable fields around were full of fieldfares and redwings, migratory thrushes driven down from the north by the cold. But the present treelessness of the Wiltshire hills is misleading; for all we know the West Kennet tomb's early days, or centuries, were spent in a forest clearing, just as there were almost certainly far more trees on the first Stonehenge horizons than we can easily imagine now. Indeed it is very possible the long stones were originally set on end to imitate, or immortalize, tree trunks. Yet the present denudation is apt; scissors cut paper, paper wraps stone, stone blunts scissors, so goes the old children's game. Megaliths are formidable waiters, and somehow their endurance is better shown by the humbler, much shorter-lived vegetation that now enisles them; the great stones, the tiny blades of winter wheat.

A patient, lonely, noble place, as Stonehenge must once have been, when one could come on it so, and touch it; feel and be felt by it.

From West Kennet we headed south-west under a blue sky for Devizes, through what is one of the nearest equivalents in Britain to a prairie; vast gently rising swells of uninhabited farm-land, all its earth-tones muted by the freckling debris of stones and chalk many thousand times shattered by the ploughshare. This immense breaking and powdering throws a kind of ghostly whitening veil over all the bare land at this season; here and there stand little squadrons of green flying saucers, ancient disc and bell burial-barrows, or tumps, that have been saved from the plough and allowed to turf over.

Devizes is one of the most agreeable old market-towns in England, and has a museum to match, as I was to find that day. Though the principal museum for the Stonehenge finds is at Salisbury, one gets a better picture at Devizes of the cultures, New Stone and Bronze, that lie behind the field monuments. One can't savour Stonehenge fully unless one goes to the two museums as well, and it is sad that only a tiny minority of the thousands who stop for an hour at Stonehenge every summer find time to make the other vital two-thirds of the visit – and even sadder that our worthy but puritanical Department of the Environment does not do anything to make the legwork less arduous for the visitor. But Devizes handsomely rewards the effort, with its cases of pottery and ornaments and golden grave-goods. Some of the latter are clearly Mediterranean in style; and there are parallels, perhaps more aesthetic than scientific, even in the megalithic monuments themselves. The extreme recent theory that the Stonehenge we know today was built by the early Greeks is now out of favour; the question of a filtered influence is another matter. I had even felt it inside the West Kennet tomb that morning, even though it long predates Mycenaean Greece: a dim yet unmistakable kinship with the Lion Gate, with certain parts of Tiryns.

An Elizabethan view

I finally left the museum cases at Devizes to go upstairs, where in a series of book-lined rooms, the library of the Wiltshire Archaeological and Natural History Society, the other and equally real Stonehenge lies. My welcome there was as helpful as the Stonehenge attendant's had been the reverse, and soon I sat surrounded by a pile of old prints and books – and by what must attract any writer or artist to Stonehenge, the extraordinary power it has always held over the English imagination. Here Inigo Jones the architect demonstrates his theory with geometric certainty and elaborate plates and diagrams; here Walter Charleton, in his florid and totally bookish *Chorea Gigantum* ('The Giants' Dance', an old name for Stonehenge and treated literally by some early artists, who show the trilithons swaying in a kind of stately conga) takes issue; and here is what I have really come for, the greatest of all the early mythmakers – and paradoxically, the closest to a modern archaeologist. His name is William Stukeley.

One of the most precious and charming possessions of the library at Devizes is a manuscript Stukeley notebook. By mistake I opened it the wrong way round and found myself reading an exceedingly grisly account of menstrual irregularities in a lady smallpox victim (Stukeley was also a doctor of medicine); but the bulk of the book consists of his field-drawings and notes of ancient remains and ruins all over southern England, and especially in Wiltshire. The drawings are in sepia and a cool grey wash, sometimes touched with little ust-red ink-lines, and are for their early eighteenth-century time meticulous and accurate – and infinitely valuable now, since Stukeley recorded many stones long ploughed under, or carted away by local farmers for gateposts, or broken up for wall-building.

Yet art and literature (and local history, the first reasonably accurate drawing of my own small town in Dorset was done by him, and the same is true of countless others) owe a debt to Stukeley for something beyond his painstaking topography. This is for the great fallacy of his life, his seizing upon an idea of John Aubrey's and magnifying it into an obsessive conviction that Stonehenge and the rest were built by the priests of the ancient Celts, the Druids. His weird and wonderfully illustrated book, *Stonehenge, A Temple Restor'd to the British Druids*, is the key to all that has subsequently become of Stonehenge in the communal imagination. He makes it very clear from the start, in the preface, what he truly intends

8

to do. 'And seeing a spirit of Scepticism has of late become so fashionable and audacious as to strike at the fundamentals of all revelation,' the old man (by then a cleric, as well as doctor and antiquarian) announces that his aim is 'to promote ... ancient and true Religion'.

Stonehenge Restor'd was first published in 1740, and must rank as one of the very earliest harbingers of the Romantic Movement, especially in its more bardlike and ruin-besotted aspect. In modern scientific terms, one can largely dismiss Stukeley with a smile, even though he was the first to note the thing that has sent the mathematicians and astro-archaeologists, the Thoms, the Hawkinses and the Hoyles, flocking to Stonehenge in recent years – that is, the solstitial alignment. But Stukeley incarnates something that remains strangely true, and unique, about the place. It is not quite like any other ancient monument in these islands, or anywhere else in the world, and that is not because of its physical self and archaeological features, though they are remarkable enough, but because of its power to challenge the imagination of its beholders. Still today it is not what we know of Stonehenge that haunts us, but what we do not and shall never know. It is like some very ancient and corrupt text, of which one can decipher just enough to be sure it is very important, but never enough to establish exactly what it is saying.

This aspect of Stonehenge was put very well for me during my own disappointing visit. I stood at one point close to a young couple who had brought their children. One of them, a small boy, was evidently better briefed than I had been forty-five years before. At least he realized the banned playground was made by man. He contemplated it for a few moments, then looked up at his parents.

'Why are there so many doors?'

Two or three weeks later I was back in Devizes, along with a packed audience of several hundred people, to hear the principal living authority on Stonehenge, Professor Richard Atkinson, give a lecture on the latest theories and discoveries concerning the monument. We listened to an eminently lucid and clinical discourse on the most recent datings of the major phases of building, on the results of the latest excavations. When this was done the chairman, the equally authoritative Professor Stuart Piggott, called for questions. There came some requests for various elucidations of technical points, which were given. Then a young man stood up at the back.

'Would Professor Atkinson care to say anything about the peoples who built the three main phases – their culture and religion?'

He might as well have asked a synod of Methodist ministers whether they would consider publishing a new edition of De Sade's *120 Days of Sodom* – or the Department of the Environment how he should apply to turn Stonehenge into a disco. All such speculation was futile, the wicked fellow was peremptorily told. Such information was strictly dependent on written records, the Stonehenge peoples did not have writing, we knew nothing, we would never know anything; to speculate on such matters was not only totally unscientific, but far worse, it encouraged the lunatic fringe. In the slightly shocked silence that followed this icy douche – though we had been warned, it had not been the first mention of lunatic fringes – Professor Piggott rose to announce that the lecture was at an end. No more questions.

It may seem from the above that I am a defender of lunatic fringes and that I think the inner sanctum at Stonehenge should be opened to the public again. In fact I have very little sympathy with those who feel chthonic spirits and magnetic field-forces, or who see ley-lines, serpent-goddesses, gigantic genitals and heaven knows what else in every ancient land-scape; who get a kick out of Stonehenge like a sniff of cocaine, or take it as a stone sedative to cure the headaches of a world too much with us; least of all do I have sympathy for the absurd modern Druids. Harmless cranks though these latter no doubt are, they seem to me to deserve all the mockery that they have received from the very first of their annual charades, in 1909.

Nor could I argue seriously against the decision to keep the public away from the central area. The same problem besets the guardians of famous ancient monuments the world over. Neither soil nor structure can bear the constantly increasing strain of tourist traffic and our loss there is fundamentally a by-product of the universal problem of our species: gross overpopulation.

Yet somehow, somewhere, in all of this I sense something that is perhaps characteristic of modern life in general, and merely illustrated rather vividly at Stonehenge. It has to do with the vaguely prison-camp atmosphere at the site, the distinct tinge of a bureaucratic assumption that ordinary people cannot be trusted near anything valuable; it has to do with the design, or rather brutalist non-design, of the new underground approach, with the absence of any related material in an on-site museum, with the coldly scientific public de-scriptions (there is in fairness a bookstall). It has to do with the austere charm, the moving solitude, the peace of the other Wiltshire sites that have not been so adamantly historicized – some only a few minutes' walk from Stonehenge itself.

Perhaps above all it has to do with Professor Atkinson's over-defensiveness before a politely asked and reasonable question, in the context of a generally lay audience. I would not be unjust. He and Professor Piggott are the undisputed *doyens* of British prehistory. Their excavations in the 1950s revolutionized our knowledge of the monument, and no new theory about it can be accepted until it has undergone their severe scrutiny. Yet there was for a few moments an unmistakable fear of giving an inch to non-science, as if it must be synonymous with nonsense; to the enigmas, however much they are at present banned from the ground, of the place.

Writers are privileged creatures in one way, since our single sincere and deeply held allegiance is to ourselves and our craft; which allows us to stand back a little. In my research for this essay, and in a good deal of magpie reading in texts ancient and modern, nothing was stranger than that moment at Devizes – or more betraying, it seemed to me, of a quite unnecessary polarity in twentieth-century society between pure science and impure speculation. Of course 'lunatics', third-rate mystics and literary hucksters do exploit this empty space between what is certain and what we long to know; but to deny all validity to such longing, to natural speculation, which is essentially to deny value to any other system or knowledge outside science, is a potentially far more dangerous lunacy. No society can live by scientific bread alone, for the very simple reason that no individual can or does exist on such a diet – and in much more important matters than the 'correct' attitude to Stonehenge and the puzzles of its past.

Some people like to see ancient Stonehenge in terms of astronomer kings, or magi, and a vulgar herd. History has had quite enough of such elitist concepts, blind worship of castes based on esoteric knowledge. One cause of the present polarity is the widespread and incipiently fascistic respect our century has foolishly accorded pundits and gurus – two of our least happy borrowings, linguistically as intellectually, from Indian culture. I am not, I hasten to add, putting Professors Atkinson and Piggott in those categories. They are true scientists.

Yet I hope there will always be a case for the lay view, even though with Stonehenge it is fraught with reefs and dangers. Any innocent approaching the subject will soon feel like the ram-in-a-thicket of another ancient culture: so many disputes between authorities, so many contradictory statements in the handbooks, so many confusions over dates ... at one point I wished I had taken the early advice of an archaeologically-minded friend, which was not to go within a thousand miles of such contentious and complex territory. At least all this made the choice of an epigraph an easy matter.

And at least I am spared the job of describing the actual appearance of the monument, since Barry Brukoff brilliantly relieves me of that duty in his photographs – which convey the presence and poetry of Stonehenge far better, alas, than any visit now is likely to. What I should like to attempt is a layman's picture of how both Stonehenges arose: the one in stone, the one in the mind – what people built it, and what it has built in people.

THE PAST

UNTIL VERY RECENTLY Stukeley was considered right in one of his general premises, if not in the particular Druid colouring he gave it: that is, that the story of Stonehenge begins a very long way off, both in time and place. Even in its first and largely stoneless phase (about 2800 B.C.) it is a distinctly late-come monument of the general civilization that preceded the Copper, Bronze and the Iron: the Neolithic, or New Stone. Because the earliest Neolithic cultures arose in the Middle East, it was long assumed that they must have spread from there. A conscious reason was the importance of the Egyptian pharaoh-list, starting at 3100 B.C., for dating, while the history of Christianity and the nature of scientific discovery provided two unconscious models for this 'diffusion' theory – the notion of a new truth arising in one place and time, and then travelling out, like the Olympic torch, to the dimmer rest of humanity.

The very earliest New Stone cultures appeared in the Middle East just after 9000 B.C., principally because of a marked warming in the world's climate at the end of the most recent Ice Age, and also because the wild ancestors of wheat, barley and flax come from that part of the world. Wild sheep and goats were available for domestication, and dogs, pigs and cattle (for meat, dairy-farming did not come for several millennia yet) soon followed into mankind's larder and service. By 6000 B.C. the Neolithic had become the dominant culture through the Middle East, with numerous settled communities and the beginnings of an agricultural technology and economy, although hunting (bow-and-arrow and sling) and fishing (hooks, harpoons and nets) long existed side-by-side with farming. It is possible planting was the women's job; hunting and animal-tending, the men's. The first crafts, basketry, leatherwork, pottery, weaving from flax, evolved with the stabler conditions.

Gradually, according to the diffusion theory, Neolithic man and woman hunted, grazed and forest-cleared their way out from this 'cradle of civilization' – and in one direction up the valley of the Danube and across Europe, arriving in Holland about 4500 B.C. and very soon afterwards crossing the North Sea to Britain. Towards the end of the fifth millennium they settled among other places at Windmill Hill, near Avebury, where they built a so-called 'causewayed camp'. The term is confusing, since some of this type of Early Neolithic structure were in fact converted by succeeding cultures into true camps or hill-top fortresses; but their original function seems unlikely to have been only that.

There is another causewayed enclosure from this remote period only three miles from Stonehenge. There are a number of theories about their purpose. Windmill Hill has provided evidence of regular meetings and ceremonial feastings and use by people from afar as well as close by, and over a long space of time. One suggestion is that it had an autumn assize-cum-market status, where surplus produce and animals could be traded and tribal or family squabbles settled. Prescribed common meeting-grounds with similar functions and a temporary taboo on violence to strangers are known from later primitive societies. We can be sure the place would have had great religious significance as well; one smaller enclosure at Windmill Hill is probably a mortuary one. It may not be too far-fetched to see these causewayed enclosures as the first faint ghosts of the civic community, or town. The difference is that they do not seem to have been regularly lived in.

Perhaps the most important technological 'leap' from the earlier Stone cultures took place with the axe. The Neolithic axe is a very impressive tool, as brilliantly developed as the innate limitations of its material will allow. I have one beside me as I write, of tough greenstone, almost ironlike in weight. Some four inches long, it dates from about the time of the first Stonehenge and comes from a famous axe 'factory' in Cornwall, though it was found in Dorset. Its edge is long blunted, but it remains a beautifully compact and perfectly balanced little object. As with all Stone Age tools one has to grip it in one's hand to appreciate its true sophistication – the subtlety of its two faces, one more convex than the other, the way the curved blunt end is designed to fit the inner side of the thumb; or how the side-edges vary, the one slightly sharper to give a purchase on the thumb-cushion, the other rounder, to make an easier grip for the fingers. Only fools judge such objects by sight alone. They may look crude and clumsy; they very rarely feel it in the hand.

Mine is a hand-axe, but others were hafted, and modern experiments have shown that they are surprisingly efficient in tree-felling, though a different technique has to be used from that with the modern steelhead axe. The axe was the indispensable tool in the dense forests of northern Europe. Widespread evidence of Neolithic clearing can be obtained by pollen-count. Tree-pollen levels drop, those of cereals and cultivated-land weeds rise.

But the diffusion theory, this comfortable notion of civilization slowly seeping westwards and northwards, received a catastrophic blow with the discovery of radio-carbon and tree-ring dating. It emerged that a number of Neolithic sites remote from the Middle Eastern 'cradle' were much, much older than had previously been believed, and that metal technology in some cases predates the supposed invention of the art in the East. Breton tombs could be carbon-dated back beyond 5000 B.C.; some Balkan Neolithic peoples had 'cracked' copper by 4500 B.C.; Varna on the Black Sea had skilled goldsmiths by 4300 B.C. The new and more plausible explanation lies in the idea of parallel evolution.

Probably the truth sits somewhere between the two theories. There is certainly evidence of a good deal of movement in the fourth millennium B.C., which was also in climatic terms the golden millennium of the last ten thousand years. We have a much better documented knowledge of another and later warm period, in the first millennium of our own era, and its effect on humans. It was not just an early *machismo* and land-hunger that launched the Viking longships; indeed those aspects of the Viking character were very arguably mere by-products of the inducement to see the world and settle elsewhere provided by the fine weather. It is difficult too to suppose that the various cultural and religious similarities among the more northerly Neolithic peoples all arose independently.

One important factor here may well have been exogamy, the practice (arising from incest taboo) of marrying one's womenfolk outside the immediate family or clan. All through history young women have been to culture rather what wind is to thistledown – great carriers of it to new places. Something very akin to this played an important part in the life of nineteenth-century rural Britain. Labouring families kept sons to work at home and sent their girls away as maids, often to towns and cities, whence they brought back a host of new ideas, fashions and tastes to their native villages. I mentioned just now that causewayed enclosures like Windmill Hill may have partly served as cattle-markets. If they did, it is more than likely – and not for the last time in human history – that daughters would have been among the livestock on offer.

We shall never know to what extent the earliest Neolithic settlers in Britain, such as the Windmill Hill people, were true pioneers: whether they found virgin land in North Wiltshire, whether they grafted themselves on an indigenous hunter population still sunk in Mesolithic darkness … the further back one goes, the scarcer and mistier the evidence is. But we do know that this pre-Neolithic 'darkness' was only comparative. A famous Yorkshire site, Star Carr, reveals the life of a hunting and fishing community of the eighth millennium B.C. Though they were still 4,000 years away from learning to farm, they were already skilled flint and horn workers and had evolved useful weapons and tools; they wore clothes, they had some kind of primitive canoe or dug-out, they had domesticated the dog, for use as hunting-hound. They probably performed animistic religious rituals, since red-deer skulls and antlers were found that had holes pierced in them as if for wearing – though this could have been just for practical hunting purposes.

What most significantly distinguished the Neolithic peoples from these earlier British natives was the importation of agriculture. The social and psychological changes farming has effected in man are incalculable. The prime need of the hunter is a supply of game, and that can be achieved in only two ways – by nomadic movement or by establishing an isolated territory, on which no other of one's species may trespass, unless he or she is a mate, or part of a pack. But even pack-hunters, like man and wolf, establish pack territory when they are not on the move. Their gods, when they reach a quasi-religious stage, as with Palaeolithic man, are the animals they hunt. From the tiger to the gentleman member of a pheasant-shooting syndicate, they cannot be socially minded. They are also appallingly wasteful of land. Stuart Piggott has estimated that the one hundred and twenty square miles of Salisbury Plain could have supported only one very small Mesolithic hunting band, perhaps no more than fifteen adults.

The sparseness of prehistoric populations is hard to grasp today. In terms of manpower needed, the tomb at West Kennet may have been put up to serve only a handful of settled families. A Victorian archaeologist calculated that the huge outer bank at Avebury could have seated 48,000 people when it was built; his modern counterparts suspect that this would have represented the entire Neolithic population of all North-west Europe. On the other hand the then uninhabitable marshy and wooded areas of Britain were vastly greater – and more dangerous, since aurochs, bear, wild boar and wolf were still in possession. Nor should we think of either the early or the later Neolithic 'invaders' as being all static crop-growers. Many were undoubtedly nomadic herders and tent-dwellers, leaving little trace as they passed; and all must still have remained partly dependent on hunting. This nomadry would not have hurt them in evolutionary terms. The survival of the fittest favours mobility, with its increased chance of hybridization.

We know they were small in stature, seldom more than five foot six tall (which is why schoolboys, not grown men, have been used in modern stone-transporting experiments); and that they carried yew bows almost as long as themselves. These were probably quite effective up to about sixty yards. Professor Atkinson suggests we might think of these New Stone-agers as gypsies, compared to the Australian aboriginals of the Mesolithic indigenes.

Even though the primitive farmer no doubt exhausted his arable and grazing land quickly, and had frequently to move on, he was a far more sedentary creature than the pure hunters. Farming means community and the trading of surplus; it turns need, both personal and general, from a daily hazard to a potential calculation – that is, it frees labour for communal tasks and encourages the growth of specialized craftsmen, a very important social development. It produces an identity of interest; it is also divisive in the sense that it introduces the notion of personal property. By its intrinsically repetitive nature in terms of ploughing, planting and harvesting seasons, it encourages ritual religious belief and a strong interest in the calendar, in a cyclical view of life. Its gods – or more naturally goddesses – are initially created from the life-giving earth and from a concern that the dominant external cycle, that of the weather (not a matter of great importance to the hunter), shall be favourably repeated. Perhaps inevitably the two most obviously cyclical controllers or donors of weather, the sun and the moon, will eventually become the symbols, or faces, of the deity.

Agriculture also encourages countless subsidiary crafts and knowledges, from architecture to animal-breeding. Instinct plays a major part in all hunting; farming is a science. In no human activity is it less wise to disregard past experience – that is, to disobey successful past rituals. It also – unlike hunting – requires prolonged daily labour. Labour in turn becomes a suitable offering to the gods; the puritan work ethic began with the first man who broke soil to sow seed. All this automatically provides a feedback of stability into a society, which in turn threatens stasis and potential tyranny. A very great mystic, William Blake, was to see this one day, and Stonehenge as its symbolic proof.

Something of the cost of this huge change in human nature, this first and major step – perhaps the best actual correlative of the Biblical Fall – from hunting to farming, can be deduced from what scattered shards we have retrieved of Neolithic life. In Britain at least, the culture does not seem to have produced great art, and not only by future standards. There is nothing remotely commensurate with the much older art of Palaeolithic man, in his cave-painting, bone-carving and the rest; and perhaps that has to do with the close association of instinct and hunting that I mentioned just now. Ritual and ceremonial art is always repetitive art, with direct observation and natural reaction trumped by tradition, social and religious requirement, and countless other non-aesthetic factors. In it always lie the seeds of academicism.

It may seem that the much finer artistic achievements of the Copper and Bronze ages that were to follow argue against this; but I think not, for in one major way the Bronze cultures of Europe turned back to the hunting ethos, which is, like art, deep-rooted in the notion of individual prowess. It is in them – another 'price' of the agricultural revolution – that we get the first unmistakable evidence of social caste, of greed for gold and land, and of the evolution of the indispensable accompanying science, organized warfare. If the best Stone Age tools are for handling wood, soil and stone, the best Bronze Age ones are for killing or subjugating other human beings – a matter in which we have made singularly little progress.

Bronze culture seems also to mark the arrival of the male deity – feminists would say of male chauvinism – in world history. In terms of Greek mythology Rhea the earth-goddess is usurped by Zeus, Poseidon, Ares-Mars, and perhaps above all by the sun-god, Apollo.

Man begins to worship male power, war, wealth, domination over 'foreigners'; above all, himself as individual. The first Bronze Age people in Britain, the Beaker folk, were markedly more entrepreneurial and 'modern' than their Stone Age predecessors, and perhaps nowhere more obviously than in the way they had themselves buried – in single graves, not communal ones, as with Stone Age mankind. But one cannot quite put all the blame on Adam. Because of the remarkable bog-coffin graves in Denmark, we know quite a lot of how Middle Bronze Age men and women there dressed – and that the women were already willing victims of an early consumer society. They wore brown woollen tunics with corded decoration, earrings, girdles with tasselled ends, hair-nets, even a pad of false hair on one occasion; one famous blonde, evidently determined to look her best at her forthcoming interview with the gods of the underworld, had a fine horn comb tied to her girdle. The men wore close caps, tunics and capes.

Present-day mystics who, more or less in the footsteps of Blake, see some profound harmony between man and nature in this period before the Bronze Culture arrived in Britain may not be entirely wrong ... though one may doubt whether it came from some conscious wisdom as opposed to a fortunate hazard of external circumstance – innocence rather than morality; and doubt totally whether an artificial return to such a primitive state of innocence is either viable or desirable today. All pasts are like poems; one can derive a thousand things, but not live in them.

Many would claim that Neolithic art did reach high standards in other parts of the world; and there is a distinct possibility that we have totally lost one important category of evidence. Despite the name we give their culture, far more of the public and domestic building of the northern Neolithic peoples was done in wood than in stone. We can safely guess they must have had considerable skill in carpentry, and for all we know it carried over into woodcarving. But all the above-ground timber of the period has disappeared without trace. We do know they had at least one ubiquitous visual symbol, the mysterious cup-and-ring motif, of spiralling or concentric circles. This is found in Malta, Brittany and Ireland in Neolithic 'temples' and tombs, and occurs quite commonly, carved on natural rocks, in more northern Britain. I was recently at one of the most famous of these ring-decorated sites, the island tumulus of Gavrinis in Brittany. Every stone upright is covered in spiral galaxies, and the final effect is almost dizzying, very like certain types of repetitive abstract decoration in Islamic art. To some these circles (blended in the more elaborate examples with triangular shapes, almost like axeheads among tree-ring sections) are sexual symbols, to some sun and moon emblems; to the mystical they show the maze of life, to the practical they are merely quarry marks. But the one thing they do not show is spontaneity or individuality, the hallmark of the finest Palaeolithic art, and of all that has followed since.

Art and religion are the two great mirrors of any civilization, and in the absence of any clear knowledge of them one is lost. Yet there broods over Neolithic Britain a slightly chilling aura (to any modern artist) of an intensely practical culture, far more concerned with expressing itself in massive feats of engineering than in any more personal way, as if what it truly wanted to impress was neither gods nor other men, but matter itself.

One principal Neolithic deity was seemingly a mother- or earth-goddess; almost everywhere female figurines and sexual symbols outnumber male ones. Various familiar animals had a quasi-divine status, and were accorded good or evil natures, depending on whether they were counted symbolic of fertility (not always very comprehensibly to us, as with the leopard cult at Çatal Hüyük) or harmful and symbolic of death: fox, wolf, jackal, vulture, scavenging pig. But perhaps the greatest difference from what the future was to bring in religious terms was the placing of divinity in the earth below man rather than in the sky above. One crucial enigma at Stonehenge is the purpose of the Neolithic circle of pits called the Aubrey Holes. The astronomers claim them as proof of sky-study; the archaeologists see them – on rather better comparative evidence – as proof of earth-worship.

We do know something of Neolithic funeral practice, and increasingly in recent years from an unexpected source – the much later Neolithic cultures of Northern America. Too many strange 'coincidences' have come to light for there to be any doubt that primitive American society contains instructive clues about British prehistory. It can be deduced archaeologically that British Neolithic man did not bury his corpses at once, but burnt or otherwise got rid of the flesh first in open-air mortuary enclosures (in Neolithic Turkey the excarnation was done by vultures). Only the bones were laid in the communal tombs; and then it seems that very often the skulls were removed again, and placed elsewhere, presumably because they had ancestor-spirit powers (what biologists call threat-display) of protection. Identical practices are known from many American Red Indian cultures.

The evidence is overwhelming in the metal cultures, from Mesopotamia to Wessex, of a belief that man could take his worldly possessions – and status – with him to a next world. This is clearly what grave-goods are for, and their general paucity in earlier Neolithic times suggests a less personally interested attitude to death. It is almost as if they saw death as something to be cultivated (once it had occurred) for the common good; while Bronze Age man took it as we do, as a private challenge. The common factor in both attitudes lies in the need to expend effort and labour over this, and religious observance generally, far beyond what is required for mere survival. It is very hard not to see the truly gigantic work-offering put in at Woodhenge and Durrington Walls, at Stonehenge, Avebury, Carnac and elsewhere, as an obsession with immortality, with defying time and death. The number of burials found inside the precinct at Stonehenge is not exceptional, but an enormous constellation of nearly 350 surviving funeral barrows stands close about.

There is some vanished (down people's throats) evidence that ancient man favoured burial much nearer to the stone circles. In 1685 a Dr Robert Toope wrote to the antiquary John Aubrey about an interesting discovery. He had chanced on it in 1678 near Avebury, at the Overton Hill Sanctuary, which excavations in 1930 revealed to have had three phases of wooden building beginning about 2900 B.C. and finally a double stone ring (long disappeared) in Bronze Age times; this latter as at Stonehenge and coevally with it. Workmen were enclosing a field there and told Toope they were digging up many bones. 'I quickly perceiv'd they were human, and came the next day and dugg for them, & stor'd myself with many Bushells, of which I made a noble medicine that relief'd many of my distressed Neighbours.' Toope says that this unexpected contribution to his dispensary was 'about 80 yards' from the outer circle of the Sanctuary. He found the skeletons lying so close 'that scul [skull] toucheth scul', and that they were set in rows, all pointing towards the 'temple'. Unfortunately he could not resist this supply of medicine and returned to his Golgotha for more bones. In the 1930 excavation the skeleton of a girl was found inside the circle, her bones ritually broken. A similar young sacrifice, with a cleft skull, was found at Woodhenge.

Death, alas, is a much better archaeologist's assistant than life, since it leaves so many more traces and clues behind it. A kind of variation of the pathetic fallacy – a mortician's fallacy – soon overcomes anyone who reads prehistoric archaeology: all seems death and disease, a brutish struggle in the nastiest of all possible worlds. Nothing is easier than to discover decayed teeth, poorly mended bone-fractures and signs of rickets in a Neolithic skeleton; to find a joy in dancing, a skill at fowling, a sense of humour, is impossible. We know not one single thing of the physical and emotional capacities, the thought-processes and sensitivities of these lost ancestors of ours. We may with an effort subtract all or most of our present culture and imagine what it would be like to live without it; but we can never begin to imagine the other side of the moon, the pleasures and rewards of the men and women who lived then. It is forever secret, undiggable, unpierceable.

I long ago formed my own view of this: that a kind of mysterious parity of recompense for existing does rule over animate nature – though not over any given individual, of course. But a major component in that recompense must always be ignorance – not knowing, or not being able to imagine, anything better. Neolithic man was far richer in ignorance than we are. If happiness in being alive is to be the gauge, we may not be quite so lucky, or they to be so pitied, as we like to think.

THE MONUMENT

FURTHER SOUTH NEOLITHIC man built his houses in stone and sun-baked brick; yet over most of his wetter range he used timber, generally erecting rectangular long-houses of split logs, sometimes plastered with clay or mud. But far more extraordinary are the great timber round-houses. One of the very earliest of this type was built soon after 3000 B.C. at the Avebury Sanctuary on Overton Hill. There is another group of them very near indeed to Stonehenge, at Woodhenge and Durrington Walls – not immediately interesting, for little has survived to see on the ground, though I recommend the six concentric and elliptical rings of cement stumps (marking the original postholes) at Woodhenge to the connoisseur of modern art. By chance the ghost of this very ancient English building is now marked out in accordance with some very advanced notions of twentieth-century sculpture.

This sudden interest in symmetry and circles came from an important new wave of Neolithic tribesmen, who descended on Wiltshire from Eastern England and gradually replaced or absorbed the Windmill Hill peoples. They seem to have been more nomadic herdsmen than true farmers in the beginning, but their most important cultural importation was the single-entrance henge (the word is derived from Stonehenge and means 'a banked *circular* precinct'), usually associated with cremated burials in pits. It is these people who built the first Stonehenge. Theirs was a native tradition evolved in Britain, with few parallels elsewhere in Europe.

The circular shape must of course suggest the sun and sky-worship, and it seems more than probable that a change towards this took place before the arrival of the earliest Bronze-agers. There was certainly a long and confused transition period. Evidence of Beaker influence on pottery appears long before the usual dates given for their main arrival on the scene, while signs that formerly unprotected native sites, like Durrington Walls, were being turned into defensive fortifications go back to 2500 B.C. Perhaps the situation was not unlike that of the sporadic Hun invasions of later history. The Beaker peoples were certainly warlike. They had a chieftain system, they had metal, they had the belief in individual as opposed to communal burial; but they evidently also shared, or took over, the native faith in the circle.

First settlers picked on Durrington Walls, beside a backward loop of the river Avon some two miles from Stonehenge, just before 3000 B.C. Of this period very little survives, but it can be deduced that the area was then wooded, chiefly with hazel-copse, but also with oak, birch, pine, lime and elm trees, and that the people began clearing it for their crops and grazing. They had flint tools from a flint mine nearby and made primitive pots. About 2500 B.C. (Stonehenge first phase, 2800 B.C.) new Neolithic settlers moved in and constructed the present Durrington banks and the internal ceremonial buildings. The huge huts, like the celebrated one immediately adjoining at Woodhenge, do not seem to have been lived in, though they may have had dwelling-houses very near. Much of the site has never been excavated, but it is known that many more buildings are there. These round-houses bear a remarkable resemblance to certain seventeenth- and eighteenth-century Cherokee and Creek Indian meeting-houses or 'rotundas' in America – which we now know have a much older history. One in Illinois has already been dubbed 'the American Woodhenge'. There is evidence at Durrington Walls from adjoining middens of either feasting or frequent sacrifice, and of the ritual breaking of pots.

The earth-bank alone at Durrington Walls would have taken a hundred men, using antler picks and bovine shoulder-blade shovels, at least two and a half years' work – and doing nothing else meanwhile. The round-houses required an equivalent effort. The major timbers were all oak, and would have needed at least nine acres of felling, quite apart from shaping, transporting (perhaps by floating down the Avon, with the backward loop forming a convenient 'harbour'), erecting and all the rest. In their complete state the great wooden buildings must have been quite as impressive as the stone henges.

But even Durrington Walls pales beside what had begun at Avebury at least a century earlier, about 2600 B.C. The Avebury men, perhaps because huge boulders of the same sarsen-rock that was later to come to Stonehenge lay close at hand, forsook timber and lined their huge circle (three Stonehenges would fit comfortably on its diameter) and its two inner rings and entrance avenues with the massive stones. Though undressed, these stones seem to have been split to conform to two models, one diamond-shaped, the other more columnar, evidence to many archaeologists of a male and female symbolism. They also dug a ditch and bank of astounding size, equivalent in shifted bulk to an early Egyptian pyramid – a labour of Hercules for which they must have got in training by putting up their own pudding-pyramid of Silbury Hill a mile or so away. They began that about 2750 B.C.

Avebury (only some seventy-six of its original six hundred or so megaliths are still in position) has suffered far more severely than Stonehenge from the ravages of time and man,

Silbury Hill by Stukeley, 1723

and is harder for us to judge in terms of enormity of enterprise. Though Stonehenge is amazing enough in this context, Avebury is more amazing still, especially as it predates the major stone phase of its rival by at least six centuries. It also raises the problem of whether such huge tasks could have been organized without some Stone Age foreshadowing of the well-attested Bronze Age power structure. One or two contemporary Neolithic graves from the area have revealed things like maceheads beside skeletons, which strongly suggest chieftain regalia.

But the present Stonehenge is basically an advanced or petrified-forest model of the neighbouring circular wooden structures inside banks. All the probabilities are that in its earliest days it also had a similar central wooden building, though no clear evidence has yet been found – or may ever be, in such disturbed ground. (The disturbance began with the builders of the various stone phases of the monument, and has continued into our own age. The major excavation of this century, in the 1920s, is now generally considered a disaster, since it destroyed for eternity almost as much as it revealed.) The huge lintels on the uprights must reproduce some internal structural feature of the wooden buildings, which were roofed and would have needed cross-strutting.

ead or halpen.

The larger posts – two of oak at one of the Durrington Walls buildings' entrances weighed five tons apiece – may also have been carved or stained with red ochre and had some totemic function. The herm, the head and bust set on a pillar, is one of the most characteristic shapes of both Greek and Celtic art, while the setting upright, against gravity, of tree-trunks and stones as part of ancestor-worship is common the primitive world over. Many other prehistoric stone groups in Britain, such as the Rollright Stones and the Stanton Drew Circles, have revealing myths of origin, in all of which man is turned into megalith. Stonehenge's ancient nickname, the Giants' Dance, implies the same thing. Once again, we know from America that dancing and wooden circles were closely associated. A famous sixteenth-century print shows Virginian Indians dancing round a ring of posts with carved heads on them.

The elliptical Woodhenge is also laid out with considerable mathematical expertise and like Stonehenge, orientated to the summer solstice in the north-east. All these Stone Age monuments give ample evidence that the later Bronze Age skill at handling huge weights and organizing a considerable labour-force was in an ancient local tradition. The sheer task of assembling and erecting Stonehenge is in no way unique; what is unique is its architecture – not that it was built, but the way it was built.

Scientific archaeology divides the building of Stonehenge into five or six phases, the first being as remote from the last as the seventh century of our era is from us today. What we now see is merely the end-product – the point where the work stopped.

Stonehenge I is the Neolithic monument, started about 2800 B.C. It consisted first of the originally six-foot bank and ditch. The latter was merely the quarry for the former, and is not even continuous. Soon afterwards were dug the fifty-six strange pits called the Aubrey Holes – named after the seventeenth-century antiquary John Aubrey – that make a circle just inside the bank. To astronomers they are unique things, as I will explain later; to archaeologists, the very reverse. Such pits, some far deeper than the three-foot average at Stonehenge, are a common feature of Late Neolithic henges. These were refilled almost as soon as they were dug, and show no evidence at all that they ever held stakes or stones. What twenty-five have been proved to hold is cremated human bones, and there are another fifty-five such burials closely associated with the pits. A very similar kind of pit, the *bothros* (in Latin *puteus*, mineshaft or well), existed in Greek antiquity. Whether the Aubrey Hole burials were pious or sacrificial, we shall never know, though the presence of definite sacrificial victims at Woodhenge and the Avebury Sanctuary may suggest the latter. Since a frequent use of the Greek pits was to pour libations to the underworld, perhaps the Aubrey Holes also represent a transition stage between earth- and sky-worship.

The isolated (and exceptionally, undressed) megalith and summer solstice marker misleadingly called the Heel Stone, outside the bank, also dates from this period. Its name comes from confusion with another stone once so named because of a footprint-like depression, and the popular derivation from *helios* (sun) is totally spurious. A central wooden structure is likely; a ceremonial wooden entrance gate to the north-east is even likelier still, since wooden post-holes have been found. Finally, four very important stones in the observatory theory of the whole, the Station Stones, were erected either at the end of this first phase or the beginning of the next.

Stonehenge II, built about 2150 B.C., has disappeared now, but it had at its centre – or was to have, for it was never completed – a double circle of eighty-two bluestones, some of whose holes have been traced spanning the line of the existing single bluestone circle. This was the work of the Beaker people, and marks the start of the Bronze Age involvement. It is also the single most famous 'miracle' of Stonehenge. The majority of these rare stones can come from only one place: a small area at the eastern end of the Mynydd Preseli, or Prescelly Mountains, in the extreme south-west tip of Wales. The rest come from Milford Haven, close by.

Bluestone was favoured also for axes and in burials; ritual chips of it were put at the bottom of two later pit-rings at Stonehenge, the Y and Z holes; a fragment was even found near the Phase I Heel Stone, and must long predate the arrival of the main 'cargo' from Wales. The stone clearly possessed a potent symbolic or 'holy' value for prehistoric man. Bluestone is in fact an umbrella name for several kinds of very hard rock. One is dolerite

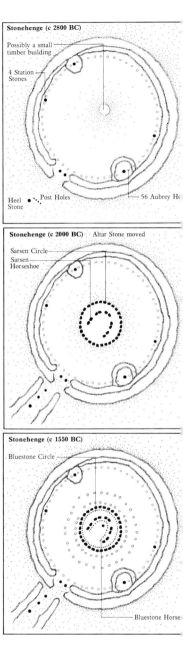

Stonehenge (c 2800 BC)

Possibly a small timber building

4 Station Stones

Heel Stone   Post Holes   56 Aubrey Holes

Stonehenge (c 2000 BC)   Altar Stone moved

Sarsen Circle
Sarsen Horseshoe

Stonehenge (c 1550 BC)

Bluestone Circle

Bluestone Horseshoe

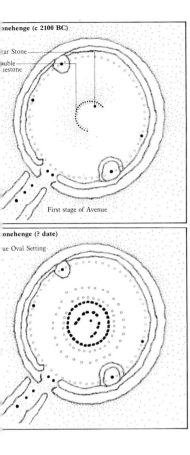

Stonehenge (c 2100 BC)

Star Stone
Double
Bluestone

First stage of Avenue

Stonehenge (? date)

Blue Oval Setting

(diabase in America), related to porphyry; another is rhyolite, related to obsidian, which was highly valued in the ancient Mediterranean – and Mexico. Indeed rhyolite and similar stones were still being made into axes well into the twentieth century by one of the last surviving Neolithic cultures, in the New Guinea highlands. In 1966 an archaeologist watched them being made. The basic rough shape was achieved with a stone hammer in only twenty minutes, but the final shaping and polishing took three weeks of hard work. Dolerite, rhyolite and three other tough Welsh stones are found at Stonehenge.

I am tempted (one dare not write about Stonehenge without introducing at least one new theory) to suggest that the stone's attraction was its colour. The Beaker peoples were sky-worshippers, and we also know blue was an important colour for an eventually succeeding culture, the Celtic. The Celts tattooed and painted themselves with the indigo-hued dye of woad, a plant they introduced to Britain for the purpose. The very word 'British' means 'the (blue-) painted Celts'; while their word for woad was *glaston* – whence Glastonbury, so important in their later folklore. Alas for my theory, bluestone looks to a modern eye more dark grey, or greenish-grey, than anything else, and it needs a strong imagination to see much blue in it. It is blue only in a medieval sense of the word, livid or leaden grey.

Yet John Aubrey in the seventeenth century did remark on the blueness of the stone when fresh, and suggested that its greyness was an effect of weathering. Professor Atkinson states that it gains 'a noticeably bluish tinge' when wet and especially where it is still polished. Possibly the fresh-tooled bluestones at Stonehenge, against the dull grey sarsens (a silicified sandstone), would have seemed bluer than we now realize. But on the whole I think we must assume that it was the hardness, or durability, of bluestone that was its main attraction; and that its comparative colour among other granite-like rocks was only a subsidiary matter, or no matter at all. Similar imported and hard stones, such as haematite and nephrite (from Germany), were found at the Avebury Sanctuary. Nor should the high location of the Welsh 'quarry' be forgotten. Preseli is the most conspicuous range in that part of Wales and sacred mountains, like Olympus and Ida, are common to many ancient religions – as too is the notion that the afterworld and paradise lie westward.

Almost certainly – modern experiment shows that each bluestone (they weigh up to five tons) requires a team of at least sixteen men per ton to be shifted on land, compared to a dozen or fewer (regardless of tonnage) on water – the 250-mile journey from Wales to Wiltshire was done by raft and dugout; the former at sea, the latter on the rivers, where the minimum 20-foot square rafts would have been too broad in the beam. Two or three dug-outs lashed together can bear the weight. The most plausible route is up the Bristol Channel and then, with one or two porterages, inland along a network of streams, ending at a point on the Avon near the site. We can date this epic task fairly closely because the first part of a crescent-shaped dragging-way from this point and up to the monument was banked about 2150 B.C. (the median date of two antler-picks found in it). The way is called the Avenue, and must represent the latest period at which the stones were brought.

Primitive sleds, probably in combination with timber rollers, and cattlehide tow-ropes were the land means. One recent theory argues that the bluestones were brought most of the way by glacial drift, but few archaeologists accept it. An older one posits an earlier bluestone 'temple' in the Prescelly Mountains, and makes the Wiltshire men precursors of the American millionaires who once used to ship medieval cloisters and castles across the Atlantic. But there is little evidence of a considerable Neolithic culture in Pembrokeshire.

As we have seen from Avebury, the glacial theory is certainly not necessary from the point of view of bulk-carrying skills. Other huge tasks of this kind – such as bringing the far larger sarsen-stones (ranging in the uprights from 25 to 45 tons) to the site – could not have been done other than by hand. Nor are the Stonehenge bluestones the only ones brought to the area. Another has been found whose arrival can be dated back to 2900 B.C., before Stonehenge was even thought of, and long before the Beaker folk. The earliest possible dating for those at Stonehenge is about 2350 B.C. The most interesting implication of this extraordinary feat is rather more its social than its physical enormity – and not only in terms of disposition of manpower, but in community relations. It is hard to imagine how such an endeavour could have taken place in an island of isolated, warring tribes.

Yet war of some kind must have been in the air, for the Beaker people were seemingly driven from Salisbury Plain before 2000 B.C. (their characteristic pottery begins to disappear a century earlier), which may well be why they never finished their double circle. Very soon afterwards Stonehenge IIIa was started by their Bronze Age successors, known in their heyday as the Wessex Culture. This is by far the most important phase in the monument's long history, and essentially gave us the Stonehenge we know today.

The unfinished double bluestone ring was put aside for re-use later, and the lintelled sarsen outer ring and massive horseshoe of inner trilithons erected. Two standing stones were put up by the entrance to the henge, roughly on the Heel Stone line. One has disappeared, while the other has fallen and become known as the Slaughter Stone – without any archaeological evidence whatever. The case of the so-called Altar Stone (actually the largest bluestone) at the heart of the stone-ring is exactly similar – no trace of a sacrificial function has ever been found, outside the romantic imagination. The Altar Stone most probably once stood upright near the central and tallest trilithon.

Sarsen derives from 'saracen', once a common English term for 'heathen'. Eighty-one of the giant stones had to be brought from the Avebury region twenty-five miles away; and

Stukeley's Avebury

the number is significant. One Sarsen, the Heel Stone, was already there, so this makes a total of eighty-two, exactly the sum of bluestones in the Beaker period. Evidently the new owners of Stonehenge were less revolutionary in their religious ideas than in their grandiose ambitions. Their origins are obscure. Some think new invaders came, others propose a native uprising against the Beaker intruders; or perhaps the culture was a hybrid evolved from the intermingling of Late Neolithic farmers and Beaker nomads. Since early farming cultures tend to worship the sun, and nomadic ones the moon, and since Stonehenge has features strongly suggesting an interest in both heavenly bodies, perhaps this last is most likely. Wherever they did come from, the Wessex people were commerce-minded. An important bronze industry developed in Ireland about this time, and the Salisbury Plain rulers were ideally placed to act as middlemen in the trade with the Continent. The proof that they developed contacts well beyond native shores lies in the countless barrows of their civilization scattered in the vicinity of Stonehenge.

Though many were clumsily excavated – sometimes more for 'treasure' than for knowledge – in the eighteenth and early nineteenth centuries, they have yielded abundant proof of a much richer and more dispersed culture than any before, with bronze and gold objects, Scandinavian amber and jet, even Egyptian blue earthenware beads. Irish and British artefacts turn up far to the south. It is the dawn of international trade, and one begins to smell embryo kings as opposed to savage chieftains, Wiltshire pharaohs commanding huge labour-forces for vast enterprises. We do not know whether the kind of changes in social structure following on the emergence of full Bronze Age cultures in Egypt and Ancient Greece were reproduced in second millennium England; but it seems probable a much more stratified society arose, perhaps along with a far less natural approach to ritual – religion starting on its long and unhappy career as servant of the powers that be.

It is also possible the successful businessmen went in for master-race policies. Today we naturally think of Stonehenge and Avebury as one small area, but in prehistory they may have been as separate one from the other as the Homeric 'kingdoms' of the ancient Peloponnesus. There are surprisingly few Bronze Age graves and remains in the Avebury area, and the great central monument there began to fall into its three and a half thousand years of oblivion during this period. It is tempting to guess that the new kings of Salisbury Plain may have subjugated the Avebury people and used both their labour and what must have been their then renowned skill at megalith handling and erection. It is even more tempting to wonder whether the long rape of the Avebury circles and avenues of undressed stones did not begin at the same time. Avebury itself would certainly have made an easier starting-place than fetching virgin boulders from where they lay on the Marlborough Downs, and there is far less sacrilege in using already sanctified stones in another holy place than in

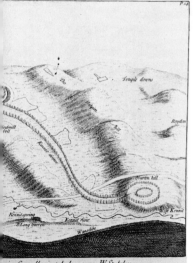

43

simply destroying them. Undoubtedly many of the larger sarsen uprights had to be sought in the field; but suitably sized material for the lintels could have been found at Avebury itself.

Slave labour or not, the bringing, dressing and erection of the sarsens is an even greater work-miracle than that of the bluestones. Professor Atkinson has calculated that the largest 45-ton monsters would have needed dragging-teams of over a thousand men; and that ten years is the minimum practical period for hauling all eighty-one stones to the henge. The logistics of maintaining and organizing such a work-force in a thinly populated countryside defy imagination. Finding the cattle-hide ropes alone must have kept a small army of tanners at work. Nor of course did the work end when the stones were assembled at Stonehenge. Sarsen is at least twice as hard to dress as granite. Flint is useless against it. It can be tamed only by itself, in the form of sarsen mauls or pounders. The soil at Stonehenge still shows an abnormally high proportion of sarsen 'sand', the result of this pounding. A modern mason using a sarsen maul was able to bang off about six cubic inches of dust in one hour. Three million cubic inches would have been needed to dress the complete circle.

Another uniqueness of Stonehenge lies here. Unlike any other comparable British monument its major stones are tooled all over (with some of the finest work on the bluestones). The best dressing on the uprights also always faces inwards, not outwards. The one exception is the great central trilithon, which is worked equally well on all sides, as if (unlike the modern Druids) the original celebrants of rites stood behind as well as in front of it.

That still left the task of getting the smoothed monsters on their feet. Their bases were bevelled for easier adjustment, and a system of sidepits used; the opposite side of the standing-hole was lined with stakes to reduce friction as the great sarsens groaned upright. They were rope-hauled, probably using two-legged gins to keep the leather hawsers above ground level and so lessen the deadweight resistance. Then they were packed with chalk and lesser boulders. The lintels must have been raised on a crib system, on successive platforms of timbers.

One other remarkable feature of this period is the carving on the uprights. The first was noticed by Professor Atkinson in 1953. He was about to photograph a seventeenth-century visitor's signature cut on one of the inner trilithons, when he realized there was a prehistoric carving just below it. The discovery of many more on other stones soon followed. The dagger the professor first saw is visible in the right light from at least a hundred yards away, and why no one in three centuries of countless visitors and close study had ever spotted it before ranks as not the least mystery of the monument.

The various carvings show axes, rectangular shapes resembling an abstract 'goddess' known from some Breton sites, and three daggers. The axes are of an Irish type from the middle of the second millennium B.C., and may be associated with the widespread Bronze Age axe cult best known from Minoan Crete. But it is the finest of the dagger carvings that is most interesting. It is narrow-bladed, strikingly like a well-known type of Mycenaean weapon (British Bronze Age daggers were broader and less angular). Since some of the grave-goods in nearby Wessex barrows show either direct provenance or strong influence from the Mediterranean, one must begin to wonder about the building.

The strongest evidence that at least someone in Wiltshire knew what was happening in Greece is in fact the monument itself. The extent to which Stonehenge IIIa is *not* like any other North European construction of its time is extraordinary. The only other European societies then achieving dressed masonry throughout, or morticed and tongued stone, or such accurate design (the sarsen circle deviates by less than four inches from true circumference, while the uprights vary only twice that tiny amount of error in their height) – in brief, conquering the rudiments of modern architecture, were the ones later immortalized by Homer in Greece. Evidence of the use of plumbline or setsquare at Stonehenge is circumstantial, but strong; evidence of considerable skill in shaping columns to allow for ground perspective is there to see for any visitor. Nothing in native prehistory accounts for this sudden sophistication – for the carrying, dressing and erection, yes; but not for the many cunnings of calculated design. And most bizarre of all, it is the only known large stone building of its entire culture.

To some this has required, to be explained, a Mediterranean overseer of works. But the only thing certain is that we shall never know: whether we owe it all to a megalomaniac but gifted Wessex Culture ruler with international connections, to a journey north by one of Daedalus's friends, to an opposite journey south by some observant native … or simply to some very original thinking at the site, which chanced to arrive at solutions close to those found in Greece. For what an artist's intuition is worth, it feels to me like the creation of one man's mind, a stroke, or series of strokes, of single genius. What he did was not to change the function of Stonehenge, but its symbolic expression. Only very great artists perform that particular kind of magic.

The two succeeding phases, IIIb of uncertain date and IIIc beginning about 1550 B.C., are of lesser interest to any but the archaeologist. In the first another bluestone setting was erected, in the second it was dismantled and then put up again in the circle and innermost horseshoe that still partially survive. Some of these bluestones were at one stage in trilithon form, like the inner sarsens. Technically there is also a Phase IV, since the remoter end of the Avenue was not banked until 1100 B.C., proof that the monument remained in use until then.

Excavations in 1978 revealed a great deal more about the site itself. The immediate subsoil is a kind of silt gathered in hollows in the underlying chalk during the Ice Age. Ancient tree-roots were found, and snail species that flourish in woodland conditions, although the immediately surrounding forest had seemingly been cleared before Stonehenge I was built, and it rose in grassland. But closely adjoining areas may have had woods much longer. Charleton heard in the 1660s that all the plain from the monument down to Amesbury had been 'a forest full of great trees within these 200 years'. No doubt the original settlers soon realized the richness of the subsoil. No ploughmarks could be found beneath the monument area, but this hazard of pockets of rich humus formed in tundra conditions explains why the region became peopled in prehistoric times.

One last associated feature of the monument is seldom visited. The Cursus, half a mile to the north, is like a gigantic but very strange athletes' stadium. Its low parallel banks are only a hundred yards or so apart, yet run for nearly two miles. They are closed at each end. These cursuses – there are several other congregations of them in Britain – were first so called by Stukeley, who decided they must be horse-race tracks. We can understand Neolithic long-barrows, we can deduce a certain amount about Neolithic henges; but their cursuses – the most famous, in Dorset, is over six miles long – remain a near total mystery. They may not even be uniquely British; a suspiciously cursus-like monument has been found near Cincinnati in Ohio, while in Peru . . . but I come to that. Most in Britain appear on low-lying ground, near water, and many seem orientated on or closely connected with long-barrows.

The Stonehenge cursus is much more ancient than the Avenue, and may even predate Stonehenge itself. It seems to be aligned on Woodhenge. A number of bluestone fragments have been found at its western end. *Faute de mieux*, some processional religious or funerary purpose is most likely. But people who feel too sure that they understand all about Stonehenge and prehistoric man have only to look north; and think again.

None of this answers the one question every visitor wants to ask. What was Stonehenge for? We can obviously grant it a religious and ritual function; the astro-archaeologists would grant it an observatory one, but this debate is far from ended. It may, as is theorized of the early causewayed enclosures, have served more secular purposes such as law-giving and judging; as a truce-ground in inter-tribal disputes; and perhaps even as some sort of annual market-place. Short of direct evidence, the analogies from early American Indian cultures may be as valuable a guide as any. The one mistake to avoid is to suppose that one function, or set of functions, must have reigned throughout. We know Stonehenge was 'active' for at least 1,700 years, and we have only to think of that time-span in our own era to realize the improbability (even allowing for a much slower rate of social evolution) of considerable changes not having taken place.

There is one other possible purpose, not only for Stonehenge, but for all these ancient monuments that stand out so conspicuously from natural landscape shape, as anyone who has seen them from the air can vouch; and this is that from the beginning they were intended to catch the attention of eyes above. Orthodox archaeologists flinch from the idea, since it issues an obvious invitation to one fiercely self-convinced section of the lunatic fringe, the believers in extra-terrestrial visitors. Yet one may dismiss the interstellar Christopher Columbuses, and still look for spectators in the sky. The degree to which primitive man personified – made things into persons – is beyond our imagining today. Even the stones at Stonehenge would have had 'souls'; and we may conclude that the sun and the moon were granted even more anthropomorphic, or anthropopsychic, being.

The Cerne Abbas Giant

Henges and cursuses might thus partly owe their forms to their effectiveness as signals – look, here are your votaries. Stonehenge itself might suggest rather more – look, we have understood some of your ways. Proof that at least one other early culture was semaphoring skywards exists in southern Peru. In a flat and almost rainless desert there the Nazca Indians (whose civilization reached back well before Christ) made huge pictograms that are meaningless and indeed unseeable at ground level. They 'drew' them by clearing areas of stones (curiously, the same rhyolite that is found at Stonehenge) on the naturally rock-littered surface. Giant condors, a giant spider, a giant lizard are laid out as if they were local earth-deities paraded for inspection before the greater gods in the azure above. More interesting still is a huge snail-shell spiral of concentric rings, of a kind very familiar from Neolithic Europe; and most interestingly of all, there are a number of very elongated wedges and rectangles. To the outer-space fanatics, these latter are U.F.O. runways; but to the less high-flying, this particular Nazcan shape must bring a very sharp recall indeed of the British cursuses. The width-length ratio of the Stonehenge cursus is about 1 : 27 and some in Peru fatten to about 1 : 9; but others there are much thinner – and they are also banked, in this case by 'hedges' of the cleared stones. Various other lines run straight as an arrow over mysterious miles. There are also religious common factors. The first conquistadors heard native stories of a schism between two cults, one of the moon, one of the sun, in which the latter had triumphed. But there are no astronomical ones: the Nazca monuments show purely haphazard alignments.

One thinks of the great circle at Avebury seen from the air, with its two inner stone circles (one of the moon-number thirty), of the very similar circles at Stanton Drew near Bristol, the largest of which is also of twenty-nine or thirty stones, and must wonder whether the constructors were not publishing an early 'Come to Britain' poster aimed at the two tourists above. Then there are the seemingly sky-tilted figures, like the famous white horses and the Cerne Abbas Giant. Though some have interpreted the Giant as a kind of scareman, designed to warn off other human intruders, he could also have been an answer to a fear of myopia in the divinities above – look, this is what we tiny ants are really like. Even modern scientists composing their radio messages for dispatch into the galaxy always include a computerized human-image diagram. And finally, so far as we know, prehistoric man never lived in the immediate vicinity of Stonehenge. It may not be coincidence that the Stonehenge cursus points at the nearest community whose existence is well attested – that at Durrington Walls and Woodhenge.

But enough of sheer hypothesis. I would now like to turn to a question that is not so frequently asked. What *is* Stonehenge for?

Woodhenge, photographed by Barry Brukoff

48

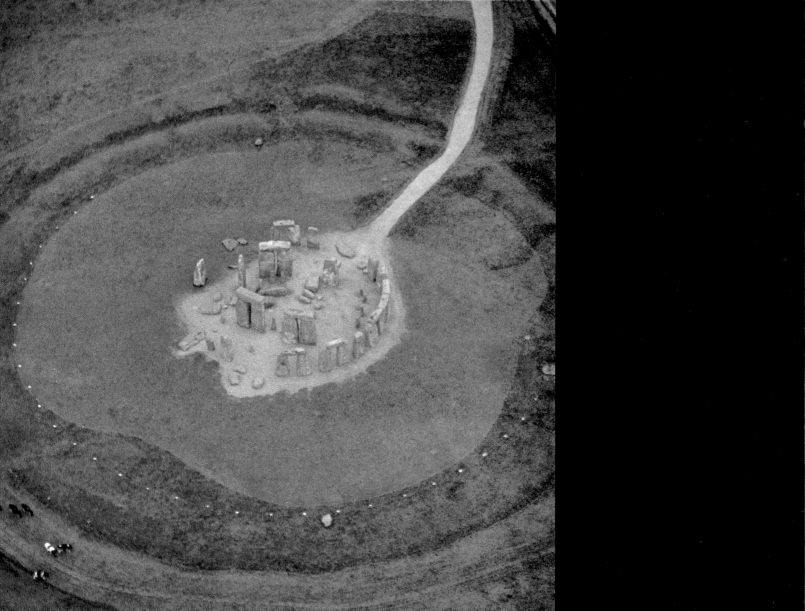

BEYOND THE MONUMENT

SCIENCE, HOWEVER INTERESTING its discoveries, however painstaking its practitioners, cannot explain the total experience of Stonehenge; the presentness of its past, the effect it still has – even in today's adverse conditions – on most visitors. That polarity I mentioned earlier does mean, of course, that there is an overwhelming pressure to see it as the experts say it should be seen, as a congregation of established facts, with a pox on all speculation. But there remains something about the place that stays, even for the most convinced rationalist, religious or shrinelike, laden with echoes and undertones for which modern life may claim it has very little time, but which linger on in all of us. You can see it in visitors' faces, an analogue of the way voices drop at the threshold of a great cathedral: a being stopped a moment, being made to think, before eternity in stone, beyond the everyday. It is, after all, the smallest, simplest and crudest of the world's great buildings, a dwarf beside the Pyramids, an abortion beside the Parthenon, a deaf-mute beside Chartres. Yet it does stand comparison, and not only because it still stands. Somewhere it manages to speak a universal.

One thing I am sure this universal is *not* is an awe of superior knowledge. Never did a building feel less like the sanctuary of some hermetic priesthood. Something like that may have come much later, with the Celtic shamans, or druids; but they do not in fact seem to have had much interest in Stonehenge, whatever their love of hermetic knowledge. I was some years ago at just such a cult place, the temple of Edfu near Aswan in Egypt. Despite its blue skies and eternal sunshine, Edfu still stinks a mile off of the dark priesthood who once lived closeted behind its unbroken fortress walls – indeed, of an ancient lunatic, or at least highly self-involved, fringe.

It is the openness of Stonehenge that is so remarkable. No ancient monument is more see-throughable, and quite literally. The six-year-old who asked about the doors made a very just observation; but it was not an original one. It figured in the very first written mention (in Latin) of the monument by Henry of Huntingdon about the year 1130: 'where stones of wondrous size are raised in the manner of doorways, in such a manner that door seems superposed upon door, yet nobody knows how or why'. And Stonehenge is a ring not merely of doors, but of open doors. It invites entry, it does not rebuff the outsider, like the Pyramids and so many other monuments to an élite caste or an élite knowledge. In some way it is porous, fenestrated like a huge stone sponge, and I believe this has a great deal to do with its power over us. Aesthetically, it is its greatest attraction. The door ajar is the oldest trick in all art, from the folk-tale to the most avant-garde cinema, and especially when mystery and eventual treasure beckon through the gap. There may have been taboos about entering the Stonehenge precinct; but there is no sign whatever that it was ever physically palisaded or walled (as it has to be now) against the common herd.

The 'doorway on doorway' effect is much diminished by the collapse of so many of the once entire ring of lintelled uprights – a collapse, as we shall see, by no means ascribable to time alone. But a clue to the other secret of Stonehenge lies in the tremendous extra effort involved in raising and morticing fast these 7-ton lintels. Each has a pair of holes carefully tailored to hold bosses on the upright jamb – they do not just perch balanced there – and each in addition is tongue-and-grooved laterally to its neighbours. Now this seems incontrovertible evidence of a determination, familiar from medieval cathedrals, to build for all time; to make sure the vertical stones will never lean or fall. We know from the Avebury circles that these early men had enormous skill in finding perfect points of balance for the huge weights they were handling; in no way a mysterious skill, but gained simply by experience and some ingenious trial-and-error techniques in filling and wedging the receiving holes for the stone-bases – and very probably in the shaping that went on before erection. But the fitted lintel would, as time has proven, provide extra security.

To my mind the most interesting thing about Stonehenge, or the Bronze Age builders of it in stone, is the growth of this obsession with durability. The desire to project one's existence, or evidence of it, beyond one's immediately surrounding generations grows transparent with the transition from wood. One vital function of art has always been to provide the means for this desire. Sheer nature is made up of brief being and infinite oblivion; and only artifice, or anti-nature, can signal escape from that process. Even without its lintels, Stonehenge is of course highly artificial in terms of ground-plan. Perfect circles are not very common in nature. But it is almost as if the builders of the present building sought for some more eye-catching artifice, some more immediate hint of the intellectual achievement hidden inside the physical, to call the future's attention. The lintel-stones not only defy gravity literally, they defy the gravity of natural oblivion. They were indeed the greatest puzzle for all the early observers of Stonehenge, like Henry of Huntingdon, who could explain their erection only by magic. The very name of the place enshrines this, for it is a kind of grim joke. The *-henge* part comes from the Old English verb *hengen*, and suggests the gallows. Stones on a gibbet, sky-hung, lynched.

All this may be seen as a first step towards what has become the dominant religion of the species, anthropocentrism – man his own god; or in biological terms as an important extension of territorial feeling, from physical to temporal space. To the sentimental it may seem blasphemous to suggest that erecting Stonehenge – or any other great building – is an activity akin to that of an animal marking its territory with its own urine and dung. But the wish to endure has profound, if not always evident, connections with the idea of property. We may take money, contemporary admiration, a thousand things as a substitute; but even today the age-old real currency, the pure gold among the lesser coinage of rewards for existing, remains immortality – or, since physical immortality remains a dream, providing evidence that one has existed.

This extension of the idea of physical territory into the domain of the metaphysical was no doubt totally unconscious in the Stonehenge builders, a 'drive' they would have understood as celebratory or placatory of whatever power or powers they believed ruled their existences; yet all that has crumbled to dust and gone irretrievably. All we are left with today is the stele, the stone epitaph of their once having undertaken and triumphantly brought off this enterprise. Whatever else is speculative or nonsensical in our admiration for the place: the farce of white-robed cranks dressing up suburban Christianity in oak-leaves and mistletoe, the silly notions of blood-stained knives over the Slaughter Stone, or of little green men dropping in to give ten lessons in instant astronomy, this remains.

We are all children of the Stonehenge builders; their compulsion, however dim and instinctive still to them in their own time, gave mankind a major new orientation, a major new purpose in existence, a major new social impetus – gave birth to all our own contemporary achievements and faults. That is why these ancient piles of stone excrement, in Wiltshire, in Anatolia, at Saqqara, in Central and South America, hold such fascination for us still.

Though we can't read it in words, a first declaration was made: man grew ambitious, and impatient with his ephemerality. Stonehenge is not simply a memorial to its Bronze Age builders; it is a memorial to a dream, and a dream still dreamt by each. Something of me shall survive.

THE MOON-MIRROR

SOME OF THE more abstruse observatory hypotheses are rather like Einsteinian theory; and well above any contemporary silly freshman's following and judgment – indeed altogether like a high-altitude fighter battle for the poor peasant on the ground ... obscure con-trails, dim explosions, mysterious grand seniors at war. At least he will eventually grasp that in the skies over Stonehenge the scepticism of some highly qualified archaeologists remains ferocious. Professor Atkinson is a case in point. One may find Hawkins, Hoyle and Thom in the bibliography of his authoritative study; but one will search index and main text in vain for any mention of their names or theories. The snub is appropriately monumental.

When all depends on alignments on significant heavenly objects and events, the main trouble occurs on the ground, or the complexity of this particular ground. Given the number of possible observing positions and 'foresights' – to say nothing of the number of heavenly objects – the freshman can at least wonder where probability ends and pure chance begins. There are other problems to do with the establishing of dead centre, in ancient times, of the stone circle. It is now known there was a shift in this between the earlier and sarsen phases of the building, and a consequent shift in alignment. Recovering what the builders would have considered *their* alignment is impossible, and especially as a method of dating the whole. The tiniest error in angle – say of one lateral inch at sixty feet – means two hundred years. Despite the many photographs that give the illusion of it, the summer solstice sun has never (in modern definition of sunrise) risen on the Heel Stone from presumed dead centre, but always to the west of it; since this solstice point is slowly moving eastwards, it would have been farther west still in 2000 B.C., and exact coincidence is not due for another thousand years or more.

The anti-astronomers do not deny, of course, that the monument is orientated – like many others – on a solstice axis; what they dispute is the historical possibility of the ingenuity and the accuracy so many of the observatory theories require to be tenable.

Some people (including Owen Gingerich, professor of astronomy at Harvard) believe the great 'scientific' phase of the monument was the first, when the observatory function and

69

lay-out were conceived and some crucial alignments taken with wooden stakes; and that the later stone phase was simply a ritual repetition, or embalming for posterity, of the empirically gained knowledge at the beginning ... just as a church is a symbolic representation of the 'facts' of Christ's life. But there is less probability of this since Gerald Hawkins's famous 'astro-archaeological' investigations in the 1960s, which suggested that the present monument was no mere souvenir of past glories, and that interest in its potentialities had survived the Stone Age into the Bronze. In an article in *Antiquity* in 1966 Sir Fred Hoyle reviewed the Hawkins theories. In the welter of trigonometry and spherical geometry a layman can only seize on the odds he gave. He suggested that in random terms Hawkins's case gave '19 heads in 23 tosses of a coin' – a chance, he added, of about one in a thousand. An unkind layman will also note that Sir Fred, a skilled writer of science fiction in his spare time, was finally so dazzled by the intellectual powers of his Bronze Age predecessors that he felt obliged to posit a freak genetic outburst.

Astronomers assume that Stonehenge was an attempt to solve some very tricky problems about accurately measuring time. If one uses either the sun or the moon alone, things very soon start going out of gear, so it was necessary to observe and understand both; and there is no doubt which is the more complicated of the two heavenly bodies, in terms of motion. We have only quite recently solved the subtler problems of the moon's erratic courses ourselves – its elliptical orbit, the fact that the centre of gravity between earth and moon is not earth-centre, the phenomenon of secular acceleration, the wobbles caused by the sun's and other planets' gravity forces, and so on.

It may seem as clear as daylight to us that the sun is the more important object in our own skies. It was not necessarily so for earlier mankind. They first of all saw time much more in monthly than annual terms. The sun may make a good hour-clock, but the changing appearance of the moon makes it a much better weekly one. It is also much more vivacious and mobile (like its nomad worshippers) than the staid old day-star. The moon dances to extremes every fortnight; the sun makes a six-month plod of it. Despite the Heel Stone and the summer solstice, one senses that the moon, or fear of the moon's powers, reigned equally over Stonehenge; one major and very sinister power it may have appeared to earlier man to possess was its ability, in eclipse terms, to 'kill' or 'eat' the sun – a power the sun did *not* possess in return.

The first major step in laying bare the moon's secrets was the realization that it works to a great cycle of 18·61 years. The Greeks had discovered that by the fifth century B.C.; but for the astronomers the intellectual miracle of Stonehenge is the evidence that its first builders had discovered it two thousand years earlier. This was not possible without a long period of empirical observation – a truly determined effort, stretching over generations, to solve the enigma. In this light, Stonehenge is far less a temple, a 'Bronze Age cathedral', than the direct ancestor of today's institutes of astrophysics.

The practical effect of the moon's capriciousness on early man is betrayed by the enormous number of superstitions connected with it, some of which most people today still vaguely feel, however commonsensical they like to think themselves. There is the taboo against seeing the new moon through glass, and the equally old belief about the virtues of turning over 'silver' in one's pocket at first sight of it. Both these notions have to do with respect. The new, waxing or full moon is generally beneficent, the waning much more connected with danger, bad augury, threat. An allied and perhaps even older superstition about the new moon held that one should spit on first seeing it – though not in contempt. Spittle was soul-material, and merely protective of the spitter, like the sign of the cross. Another has made it a dangerous act ever to point at the moon in any phase. He who pointed nine times was certain for Hell. The taboo against seeing the new moon through glass derives from folk-beliefs about ways of predicting the future by looking at the moon through glass or in a mirror; and perhaps, before glass, from beliefs, akin to those about pointing, that the moon should be looked at only by means of its reflection in water. All these superstitions indicate the same thing: man proposes, the moon disposes. It is not to be treated lightly.

There is a ubiquitous European bird, the magpie, that has also gathered some surprisingly powerful and long-lasting superstitions about itself. I was recently transcribing seventeenth- and eighteenth-century churchwardens' accounts from the village of Uplyme, in East Devon. In those days parish vestries paid bounty money for killed pests. Foxes, badgers, hedgehogs, polecats, stoats, weasels all fetched their shillings and pence. Among birds there was an immense slaughter of the magpie's near relative, the jay; but not once is bounty paid for a magpie. Yet strangely, in later Christianized folklore the magpie is generally a devil's bird, a witch bird, and one might think it doubly qualified for killing. But once again it was customary to spit for protection on seeing it; and the most revealing superstition concerns its predictive power, according to the number seen.

> One sorrow, two mirth,
> Three a wedding, four a birth,
> Five Heaven, six Hell,
> Seven's the Devil's own sel'. [self]

Analogous superstitions, to do with the number of moon reflections seen in a mirror, or in water, were used by girls to tell how many months or years away their marriage was.

Though I think folklorists have not previously noted this, I am pretty sure the black-and-white magpie is an ill-omened wane-moon or eclipse bird, and has been given the ancient moon-powers. The bad name it gets in Christian legends – cursed because it is only in half-mourning for Christ's death, and so on – is really to do with the church's long propaganda war against earlier pagan beliefs. The full moon itself suffered in exactly the same way in Christian hands. If it came on Christmas Day, it meant a bad harvest; on a Sunday, bad weather. But the church had clearly still not converted the minds of the Uplyme vestries – nor has it my own, for almost every year I let magpies do something no intelligent twentieth-century ornithologist, aware of the havoc they commit among smaller birds, would permit. I allow a pair to breed at the bottom of my garden.

This may not do me much good, since I wage war on another moon-creature – and one for whose symbolic meaning to early man there is, unlike the magpie, sound archaeological evidence as well as that from superstition. In the 1930 excavation at the Avebury Sanctuary anomalous quantities of snail-shells were found, and of species that do not live in dry chalkland conditions, but much wetter ones; in many cases they appeared to have been ritually deposited in stone and post holes. Similar finds have been made at other sites. The visual potency of the snail – and perhaps especially the common and very pretty dark-banded *Cepaea nemoralis* – has clearly to do with the spiral pattern of the shell, which provides a striking natural shorthand for the maze, the female genitals, the moon-cycle and a model for the frequently carved cup-and-ring motif of more northerly Britain and elsewhere in Europe – and indeed even for the architectural shape of so many Neolithic ritual buildings.

There are many superstitions that involve treating the snail with the same sort of respect as the magpie: greeting kindly, protecting it, reading the future by means of its trail of slime – or being told the future by finding it in one's path, which meant at least rain, and often bad luck as well. It remained, well into the present century, a part of folk-medicine in both Britain and the U.S.A., especially against chest complaints that involve excess mucus or sputum. This is because of its association with water; and that returns us once again to moon-power.

The deepest powers of the moon concern lunacy and water ... or personal and social destiny, mind and weather. Two full moons in May mean rain for a year and a day; Swithin (allegedly born very near Stonehenge) and many other European patron saints of the umbrella are simply Christianized forms of much older beliefs. Countless agricultural and domestic activities, such as clothes-washing, animal-killing and seed-planting, were once carefully geared to the moon's phases. Until very recently housewives in Britain always did their main laundry of the week on the moon's day, or Monday. The generally favoured period for sowing was just before or after the full moon, so that the seeds would germinate, then show and grow 'with the new'. Sowing at new moon was too late, and bad. Wane-moon marriages and babies were not auspicious ones (best to be born with the new moon, to move house then, or to set out on a journey). However, weaning a child was to be done at moon-waning time. The two words are related etymologically, and the white milk should dwindle with the lit crescent. Medicinal blood-letting, well after Harvey, was also dictated by waning moon-phase, owing to the belief that human blood, like the sea, was tidal.

The word *moon* is Indo-European in its roots. Our own version of it stems from the Old Teutonic *maenon*, usually supposed to be a derivative from a root *me-*, meaning 'to measure'. The oldest sense of 'moon' is probably just that: 'the time-measurer', or month. But it is not at all certain that Stone Age man would have regarded the moon as female. It is male in Norse mythology, it used to be male (masculine in gender) in Anglo-Saxon and remains so in modern German (where the sun is feminine). Slavs, Arabs and ancient Mexicans also grant or granted it masculinity. The first builders of Stonehenge, on their mother earth, may have seen a tyrannical male power – a much grimmer 'man in the moon' than that of our nursery rhymes – lying above her at night, and a female friend by day. Unlike the moon, the sun warms, and warmth is the oldest attribute of the maternal.

Finally, and perhaps most important of all, nothing is more obvious than that the kingdom of the moon is night. In daylight it is a wan ghost; at night it rules all, and night is also the domain of death. In its most northerly risings and settings near the sun's winter solstice, the moon crows over the southing star and its ever shortening days. All through the year it visibly tugs the sea this way and that. It is a hunter, as was the cold goddess the Greeks and Romans attached to it, Artemis-Diana; and we can be fairly sure that for Neolithic farmers 'hunter' must have had something of the same connotation as 'Apache' for American pioneers. A number of their skeletons have been found with arrowheads embedded in them. Male or female, the moon has an unpredictable temper, and it can hurt.

We dismiss primitive superstition rather too easily, forgetting that whatever wrong deductions it may draw it is in many ways based on a much closer, and finer, perception of natural phenomena than we possess ourselves, and a much greater need to explain them. As I write, I read of fourteen years of statistical research done by an American psychiatrist into the correlation between criminal violence and moon-phase, which does not at all obey the notion that lunacy at full moon is an old wives' tale; but on the contrary shows significant clustering of murders and assaults at times of moon-caused maximum gravitational pull. I think in this field it remains an open question whether or not early man was quite so superstitious as we choose to believe; he may simply have been a shade more observant.

Both sun and moon had to be known to establish a satisfactory annual calendar. This would not have been needed for strictly agricultural purposes, since abundant natural clocks exist to dictate the farmer's working-year to him, if that is all he needs. Correct moon-phase sowing was no doubt important, but he would not have needed Stonehenge just to get the timing of that right. What he would have wanted to know were the two pairs of solstitial and equinoctial dates, climaxes of the four seasons, for it would be a very unusual primitive culture that did not annex ceremonies of thanksgiving, sacrifice and invocation to them; and these in turn may have had attendant days for markets and settling disputes. Yet even this seems to me a minor consideration. Stonehenge must be more than an early form of executive's, or priest's, diary. The dominant thing in prehistoric man's life was weather, an immeasurably greater arbiter of human destiny than it is now, and the attempt to predict and control that must have been a principal purpose of the astronomy.

The fact that the sun, and even less the moon, do not run on fixed courses (the very fact that they appear to move at all) must have suggested that they had human attributes and so were susceptible to being propitiated, above all to being known. In addition, their changing daily natures, their travelling, their frequent – in Britain – sulks and invisibility even when they are overhead; their longer-term behaviour, the sun approaching winter solstice, the monthly death of the moon, the inevitable night – except in Ultima Thule – of even the longest and most azure summer day, the seeming 'conflict' between the two in many of their phenomena, the difference between solar and lunar years ... all this must have represented a constant threat of withdrawal and death, or at least of a precariousness in the natural order. It is not for nothing that almost all theologies are also theomachies, or gods at war.

Whatever else we do not know about a universal creator, we can deduce that he, she or it has a passion for the theatre. One of the most cunning hesitations, or moments of suspense, in all drama (and cosmic creation) is the way in which the sun at its solstices – in the periods astronomers call standstills – appears to dither. Primitive men would have been intensely more aware of these breathless pauses, when all seems to lie in the balance, than we are. Above all the drop in temperature during the winter, the evidence in nature all around, must have made the hesitation at the dark solstice a time of foreboding – and hope that the sinking sun would once more draw back from the brink of extinction.

Midwinter, or the November entry to it, has always been the most deeply felt of human festivals, because it is nearest the metaphysical truth of our condition, the day when warmth will depart from us. No one knew this better than the early Christians, when they took over the idea for their own most celebrated feast day. The presents we give then are in their deepest significance in honour neither of Christ nor Mammon, but thanks to the promise of survival in the re-ascendant sun. Nor are we in Britain burning only that Jacobean parliamentary reformer Guy Fawkes and his master the Pope on November 5th; the ritual mid-winter bonfire – and perhaps the sacrifice – is something that goes back far, far beyond the first celebration in 1606.

It is also possible that in thinking of the Heel Stone and the summer solstice sunrise, of the monument 'pointing' towards the north-east, we are quite literally taking hold of the wrong end of the stick. If we look down the axis the other way, we are in fact aligned on the winter solstice sunset in the south-west. Now the entrances to both precinct and the stone circle are undoubtedly to the north-east, and it was long ago pointed out that nowhere in the world does one go into a religious building, then turn at its centre to look back and worship in the direction by which one has entered. This 'magic' axis-line may point at mid-winter death quite as much as at midsummer joy, and it would be more reasonable to assume, on the theory that the object of deepest worship always lies *opposite* the entrance door, that the moment of midwinter death was of deeper significance to the builders. It certainly was to those of a roughly contemporary Egyptian wonder of the world, the temple of Amun at Karnak: that was aligned on winter solstice sunrise. On the other hand, the open ends of the trilithon and bluestone horseshoes do face north-east; and perhaps ancient man, like modern, preferred to turn his back on what he feared most. At least we can say Stonehenge is most human of all in this, aligned as it is on the triumph of the sun and its deepest defeat, the point where the great annual pendulum always threatens most to swing off its hook.

Such orientation is of course another thing Christianity borrowed from the past, though its churches (such as the other and more literal Wiltshire cathedral at Salisbury) chose the time of resurrection, the sunrise at spring equinox. Most old churches point there, not at Jerusalem, as the pious like to believe.

The evidence for very early precise observation at the monument, long before its stone phase, is not visible now. It lies below ground in six rows of post-holes that span the ditch at the north-east entrance to the henge. Looking from stone-circle centre they are just left of the Heel Stone, which lies slightly beyond them. To astronomers they are clearly there (Atkinson: 'Their purpose is entirely unknown') to mark six sequences of annual most northerly moonrise points during the eighteen-year cycle, so equally clearly they were observed over six cycles, or for more than a century. The Heel Stone itself could have served a double purpose – it marks not only the summer solstice sunrise, but the midswing point of the moon's varying winter risings in its eighteen-year cycle. That the two coincide is a function of the latitude of Stonehenge. There is a growing belief that this and other 'gifts' of the precise latitude may have a great deal to do with the original choice of site.

One important consequence of having got the sun and moon calendars in gear is the at least theoretical possibility that it might then have been possible to predict what must have been the most terrifying of all sky events to early man: the eclipse. So another bee in the astronomers' bonnet is to demonstrate that the monument could have served as an early warning system of the phenomenon. If it did, it must sometimes have mysteriously (to its builders) failed. Though an eclipse would have taken place, it would not have been visible at the latitude of Stonehenge.

Another potential astronomical wizardry of the monument has to do with the fifty-six Aubrey Holes, dug in the first phase, just inside the henge bank. They are in a circle (of about 95 yards diameter), beaded precisely 16 feet apart along its circumference, from which their maximum deviation is less than two feet. The greatest spacing 'error' between each two holes is also under two feet. Again the anti-astronomist will say, So what? As I explained earlier, this type of pit is very commonly associated with similar henges, and its general ritual function is well-known; that the Aubrey Holes are present is far less surprising than if they were not. Yet here the struggling layman may fancy the astronomer's side. What they have seized on is the number of pits, which is *not* reproduced elsewhere. Sir Fred Hoyle has also pointed out that the diameter of their ring is about the minimum practical one for the (by modern standards, very crude) degree of accuracy the ancient astronomers would have needed; and suggested that the length of their 'experiments', spanning generations, would also have required some permanent and unshiftable 'reference standard'. A smaller, more fragile model would not have done. Following Hawkins, he also proposed that the holes had a protractor function, and so served for eclipse prediction. But why that precise number of fifty-six holes?

The Metonic cycle of the moon takes 18·61 years. Early man, thinking in whole numbers, would have had trouble with the fraction. Yet if you multiply the cycle by three, you miss fifty-six by a cat's whisker. The difference between five solar years and five lunar ones is even closer to the same number; at first decimal level it is exact. Then the average angular distance between any three of the spaces between the Aubrey holes is 19·29°. The average yearly angular change of the moon's nodal cycle is 19·34°. The angular difference (as recorded by the ancient alignments) between maximum and minimum winter moon-settings is 19·26°. A chord of 19·26° is one third of a circle radius. Further geometrical and astronomical properties, and other ways of marking out a circle, and determining its diameter, can be derived.

In 1966 a new set of wooden foresights, quite apart from the long known Heel Stone and moon-markers to the north-east, were discovered to the north-west, in the monument's present car-park. They seem to have been intended for use from the four Station Stones, which date from the end of the third millennium. These remarkable stones are – or were, since only two survive – set in a rectangle just inside the bank and on (though later than)

the Aubrey Hole ring. To the anti-astronomists they are to be interpreted as survey points used in laying out the Phase II bluestone circle – their diagonals cross at dead centre of that monument. But the evidence that the Station Stones were far more than mere building aids is overwhelming. An observer standing at any one station and aligning on any of the other three will strike astronomical gold in almost every direction in terms of both sun and moon extreme positions, in both summer and winter. Among other things the Station Stones might have helped make a calendar. The alignment from the north-west station to a now vanished stone near the entrance gives the spring and autumn equinoxes, and the four quarters of the year could have been split again into eight 'months'.

This particular neatness and frequent right-angle aspect in the major alignments is once again a property of the latitude. Even with modern instruments the site can be faulted in terms of the truly perfect right angle by only a few miles. It should strictly have been a little further north, if this was the guiding factor in the choice of the site. But its extreme closeness does suggest more than coincidence, and that Stonehenge might also have represented some sort of astronomical omphalos, navel or earth-hub, and was consequently to be sanctified, as at Delphi in Greece. We can be quite sure that the four Station Stones pre-date the present monument, since it blocks their diagonal sight-lines and effectively makes them useless.

Finally the outer sarsen-circle stones number 30 (the same as at least one of the inner circles at Avebury). That is the nearest whole number to the synodic lunar month (full moon to full moon) of 29·53 days. Two more series of holes from Phase IIIb, like the Aubrey ring though closer to the stone circle, and known as the 'Y' and 'Z' holes, total 59, an even closer number to two lunar months, or 59·06 days. There may also once have been a ring of 59 bluestones inside the stone circle; and there is an even deeper possible relationship between the 56 Aubrey Holes and 59. The difference between 56 'tropical' years (sun-years of 365·24 days) and 59 eclipse years (of 346·62 days) is less than three days – in over 20,000 of them. Lastly, a horseshoe of bluestones at the centre formerly numbered 19, the nearest whole number to the moon's long cycle of 18·61 years. In this aspect the monument resembles nothing so much as a gigantic mnemonic system, very skilfully designed to deal with the vagaries of the night planet.

Part of the archaeological scepticism is justifiably caused by the way astronomers tend to ignore the known nature of the primitive mind and primitive religion, and especially when they transfer the ethos and aims of modern astronomy – the seeking of knowledge for the sheer abstract love of it – back to some hypothetical set of 'scientists' in the third millennium B.C. We need to imagine a much more practical concern for survival, a *fear* of the consequences of not understanding the nature of the sun and moon. Another vital consequence of the rise of agricultural society was the need for security: both ensuring the future and insuring against it. A farmer has constantly to think and plan ahead. In ancient times he might be very hungry at midwinter, but he (or more probably she) knew very well the consequences of breaking into next year's seedstock. Nothing is swifter than the arrow's flight; nothing is slower than the growth of an ear of corn. Lapse of time makes the farmer infinitely more vulnerable than the hunter, and the cereal farmer's greatest skill lies in his finding means to outwit the arch-wolf of this world: the weather his crops have to grow in.

Primitive peoples rarely think in terms of a hostile universe, but much more of a universe in their own image. Everything, animate or inanimate, has soul and personality, like themselves. If they give their deities attributes of pleasure or anger, they are only personifying what they feel themselves before the accidents of life. If I like roast meat and barley-beer, so will my god; if I like my wishes to be known, so will my god; if I can suffer, if I can remember, if I can plan ahead, so can he or she; and perhaps above all, if I like to be understood, then ... All religion is based on the notion of appeasement of a higher power and no other type of building, except the tomb, has been so persistently designed and constructed to endure, as the religious. A temple or church in decay is an insult to all gods, while buried very deep in our ideas of divinity is the notion of punishment for those who fail in respect. I said earlier that at Stonehenge man grew tired of his ephemerality; but the driving force behind the Bronze Age builders of the stone monument may well have been the belief that the gods themselves grew tired of man's ephemerality ... especially of his buildings in wood, that could warp, rot and burn so easily. The universal 'magic' tree of ancient Europe was the oak; and oak-wood is the nearest to stone.

All those quasi-romantic theories that propose a caste of nomadic wise men, setting up observatories wherever they went, seem to me tainted with druidism. The aligned rows and circles all over Britain and Brittany arose from a shared culture or corpus of belief and a shared fear – or need to prove to the powers above that the helots below were doing their best to understand them and forestall their anger. In that sense Stonehenge is like a book, an equivalent of print as information-storage system. But I think it should be seen as closer still to a tool, a metaphorical extension of plough and hoe and sickle, and whose function was the correct cultivation of the gods. The magic and the mysticism are a patina of later time.

It should surely not matter to us that the tool was misdesigned to the extent that it was conceived to answer a belief we know (or strongly suspect) is false – the notion that a deity is there to be placated and controlled; or that it finally gave rise to all sorts of less desirable superstition. Superstition is in any case a form of hypothesis, and the bedrock of all scientific advance is hypothesis. Stonehenge is in no way unique in that its greatest 'scientific' achievement may have lain in the discovery of facts about sun- and moon-motion that we no doubt profoundly secondary to the builders' real hopes and intentions. Most of human knowledge has come in the course of trying to prove false hypotheses.

I spoke of the subtleties of my little greenstone hand-axe, of its striking functionalism once it is held in the hand; and I think this is what is most attractive and admirable in the notion of Stonehenge the observatory – the quite exceptional neatness of its solution to a complex functional problem. A good test of any tool's lasting worth is the balance between simplicity of design and the number of jobs it can do. By any standards there, Stonehenge passes: and will always pass, to the end of time. Nor, surely, dare we fault those distant ancestors of ours for trying to control their own destinies. There is very little evidence that the more sophisticated gods (most of whom we no longer call gods) we have invented in the place of their moon and sun are any more likely to answer the implicit prayers we put into the building of our own Stonehenges. Their basic premise was wrong, but so still is ours. Only the endeavour is good, and necessary.

Stonehenge by Turner

THE OTHER STONEHENGE

THE RECORD OF the other Stonehenge, the dream-temple and polyvalent symbol of the scholars, poets and artists, begins – characteristically – with an account that is both false and true. It appears in Geoffrey of Monmouth's *Historia Regum Britanniae* (History of the Kings of Britain), composed not later than 1139, and makes Stonehenge an epitaph (in Caxton's words 'a monument of stone that might endure to the world's end') to British (Celtic) nobles treacherously killed there by the invading Saxon, Hengist. Stan-hengest, Hengist's Stones, was one seventeenth-century guess at the etymology of Stonehenge.

According to Geoffrey, who (a true Celt) is more famous for fiction than fact, the original idea came from the fifth-century Celtic king Aurelius Ambrosius – the nearest town to Stonehenge, Amesbury, was formerly spelt Ambresbury – but he shrewdly took advice of the Welsh magician Merlin, who told him that just the thing already existed in Ireland. Some ancient giants had brought stones with them from Africa and set them on Mount Killaraus or Killare. This may or may not be a miswriting for Kildare, near Dublin; in other versions the word is written Kyan, Kylian, Killomare and so on.

Ambrosius dispatched an army under his brother Uther Pendragon to steal them. They managed to beat the Irish, but were beaten by the stones themselves. They could not shift them, as on another contemporary occasion they could not shift (shades of a dagger carved on stone) a great sword stuck fast in a rock. Evidently Pendragon's son, one Arthur, and future king, was too young for the Irish raid. Once again Merlin was called in, and he duly did the trick. So Stonehenge came to Wiltshire. At last the slain nobles had their mausoleum; and a little later Ambrosius himself and Pendragon joined them there.

Geoffrey also records the belief in the healing and prophylactic virtues of the stones ('for in these stones is a mystery'), which lasted well into the eighteenth century; since most of the folk recipes for Stonehenge medicines and baths required pounded stone, we are perhaps fortunate to have anything left to see at all. We certainly shouldn't, were the stone not so hard. The encyclopedist Benjamin Martin complained in 1755 that 'Great Injury has been

From a fourteenth-century manuscript. The building of Stonehenge in A.D. 483

done to these Stones by the unaccountable Folly of Mankind in breaking Pieces off with great Hammers'; then adds almost in the same breath, 'I was obliged with a Hammer to Labour hard three Quarters of an Hour to get but one Ounce and half.' I can forgive Martin, since I own one of the beautiful little Gregorian telescopes he manufactured; but suspect that the gentlemen *curiosi* of the time (above folly, of course, since they were scientists) were almost as much a hazard to the monument as the hypochondriacs. Hammers for removing one's personal souvenir could be hired in Amesbury well into the nineteenth century.

In fact a far greater danger was the stone-hungry farmer. Stukeley saw much of the Avebury Sanctuary destroyed in this way in 1724. The Avebury men had long known how to split the stones. Aubrey gave their trick: 'Make a fire on that line of the stone, where you would have it crack; and after the stone is well heated, draw over a line with cold water, & immediately give a knock with a Smyth's sledge, and it will break, like the Collets [moulds] at the Glass house.'

Though not mentioned by Geoffrey another famous piece of Stonehenge folklore almost certainly dates from this same period: the uncountability of the stones. The earliest Arthurian legend has a similar feature – the tomb of Arthur's son cannot be measured. Every seventeenth-century visitor took a rather revealing – of how little science had stepped free of superstition – pleasure in proving this legend nonsense ... though not always easily. In 1651 Charles II, despite being on the run after the battle of Worcester, found time to try his hand at it. A year later a studious young Dutchman, Lodewijck Huygens, found himself at 'Stonewich' (an attempt to reproduce what was for centuries the popular pronunciation, more usually spelt Stonage, from a belief that the etymology was 'stones set on edge'). 'Everyone here', Huygens writes in his diary, 'believes the stones cannot be counted, which yet I find false, for having tried five or six times in vain, I finally arrived at the same total two or three times in succession. There are 89.' He was losing his labour. A hundred years later Martin reports that 'Numbers of daily Visitants are constantly employed' in stone-counting. His own tally was 140.

But what is interesting in Geoffrey's highly Celticized account is the survival of some pristine memory of the stones being brought to Stonehenge from the west. The African connection may be an ancient travellers' tale, a parallel drawn with similar huge trilithon erections (actually Roman olive-presses) in Southern Spain and North Africa. The notion of the sacred mountain is widespread in the ancient world – as also is that of giants. Furthermore Geoffrey may have had some justification for confusing an Irish provenance and the actual one in Pembrokeshire, since South-West Wales was invaded and settled by the Irish in the third century A.D. The mysterious 'Killare' could refer to some place in, or forgotten name for, the Prescelly Mountains, from which the bluestones really came.

This account, which is in kernel a good deal nearer the truth than many later theories, was repeated by all other medieval historians, and perhaps most charmingly by Robert Mannyng, who lived at the beginning of the fourteenth century. He composed a rhymed version of a chronicle, partly based on Geoffrey's, that had been written in barbaric French by the Yorkshireman Peter Langtoft. Mannyng was no historian, but a not unimportant figure in the evolution of colloquial English – in his phrase, he wrote 'in simple speech for love of simple men'. Ambrosius likes the idea of this ready-made cenotaph, the *Chorea Gigantum* or Giants' Carol (round-dance), waiting in Ireland, but who will bring the stones to him in Wiltshire? Merlin replies. 'Quayntise' means supernatural cunning, or magic.

> Quayntise overcomes alle thing.
> Strength is gode unto travaile,
> There no strength nor sleight will vail ...
> There you nay shall with strength
> Remove them a stone length.

When the army of removal hands was at last before the Giants' Dance, there is a distinctly comic description of military men badly in need of a backroom genius.

> These Britons ranged about the field,
> The carol of the stones beheld.
> Many times they went about,
> Beheld within, beheld without.
> All they said, so said the king,
> They never saw so strange a thing.
> How they were raised they had wonder
> And how they should be brought asunder ...
> Ropes to draw, trees to put,
> They shoved, they thrust, they stood astrut,
> One each side, behind, beforn
> And all for naught their travail lorn ...
> Yet stirred they not the smallest stone.

Fortunately Merlin was at hand to organize a more successful operation. A certain dry scepticism is already apparent in Robert Mannyng, and it grew during the fifteenth and sixteenth centuries. But by a familiar irony in human affairs, in quite rightly throwing out the fabulous bathwater of Geoffrey's theory, the early scholars were also losing the baby – the near truth about the bluestones. The great Elizabethan antiquary Camden noted that 'To think they were brought hither out of Ireland by Magick, were doting impiety, when the like stones, for greatness and graine, are found at Avely [Avebury] and elsewhere.' But he was then obliged to invent a new explanation – that the megaliths were artificial, fired together in a kiln from smaller material. The dawn of serious archaeology had come, though it was to remain for many years a largely bookish matter, much more attached to ancient texts, tortuous etymologies and obscure literary references than to actual observation.

If the dawn can be assigned to any one year, it is 1620. James I was staying at Wilton nearby, and caught the Stonehenge mania; his friend the Duke of Buckingham commanded a first excavation to be made. According to John Aubrey the principal achievement was to collapse one of the uprights of the great trilithon. Some think this must have been the eastern jamb, stone 55, which still lies fallen and broken; yet in two of his plans Aubrey carefully marked the victim as stone 56 – the westward upright, the single largest monolith ever erected in Britain, and still the most photographed. To confuse confusion he said it was 'out of the ground' in his own time; but we know such was never the case and also that this thirty-foot monster had been leaning since at least 1574. Perhaps Buckingham's men tilted it even further, to the position in which it lay until 1901, when it was set vertical again. Evidently serious damage was done and this may be why Aubrey later ignored a command from James's grandson, Charles II, to dig at Avebury. Buckingham's reward was little more than some 'old bones'. Mercifully James then encouraged another of the court circle to make a less harmful investigation. This was his famous architect, Inigo Jones.

Inigo Jones

Though Jones never completed his notes and plans, they were done up and published posthumously in 1655 by his pupil and son-in-law, John Webb. Jones was less cautious than Camden, who had thought the structure Celtic, though he did wonder whether the thirty stones of the outer sarsen circle did not 'allude to the 30 encounters that Vespasian, sent by Claudius, had with the Britons'. For Jones, 'the most notable antiquity of Great Britain, vulgarly called Stonehenge' was incontrovertibly Roman. Eight years later another royal protégé – whatever their deficiencies elsewhere, the Stuarts cannot be faulted as patrons of archaeology – Charles II's doctor, Walter Charleton, announced, with a grave twirl of largely irrelevant learning, that 'this prodigious Fabrique ... this forgetfull [forgotten] heap' must be a Danish court-royal. Webb flew to the defence of his old master and in 1665 published a *Vindication*, full of scorn and invective (in the best scholarly tradition) for the horrid doctor and his beastly Danes.

These three books, re-issued as one in 1725, mark the beginning of the modern history of both Stonehenges, archaeological and imaginative. The latter side of it was helped by a remarkable engraving in Aylett Sammes's *Britannia Antiqua Illustrata* of 1676, an un-forgettable ikon of barbaric and 'sacrificial' Stonehenge, derived from a sentence in Caesar's *Commentaries* about the Druids: 'they make hollow images of vast magnitude, with twiggs wreathed about together, whose members they fill up with living men'. *The Wicker Image* has haunted Stonehenge ever since; Wordsworth remembered it in *The Prelude*. There was also an early plate of a white-bearded Druid in the book, and yet another theory – that the builders were Phoenicians.

From Aylett Sammes's
Britannia Antiqua Illustrata,
1676

The true irony of this sudden burgeoning of the bookish and intellectual approach, Stone-henge in the mind rather than Stonehenge on the ground, is that it was scientifically absurd and yet infinitely beneficial to the actual monument. Today we know its secrets could have been unlocked only by digging; Jones and the others thought it could be done by ichnography (drawing ground-plans) and erudite speculation ... a delusion for which we may be pro-foundly grateful. If the seventeenth century had chosen to be truly empirical in its methods, it is very unlikely that we should have had much left to look at. Many more debonair Dukes of Buckingham must have ended in a heap of fallen rubble. Intellectual history has strange wisdoms, and not least in disobeying its own logical consequences.

But during all the controversy, not to say acrimony, that these books caused a far more important early investigator and first true archaeologist was at work, once again partly in-spired by Charles II. John Aubrey had first seen Stonehenge in 1634, at the age of eight. It seems it was not until 1649 that he saw Avebury. It made a deep impression on him, partly because he saw a similarity between an old spelling for the place, Aubury, and his own name; but much more because he recognized both its importance in itself and its rele-vance to Stonehenge, which then totally overshadowed Avebury in fame. In effect he virtually discovered Avebury for the rest of antiquarian England. Charles II came to see it with Dr Charleton in the 1660s. Aubrey showed them round, and climbed Silbury Hill with the king. He received strong royal encouragement to publish, but he was a hopelessly ill-organized man, and his book *Monumenta Britannica* (originally titled *Monumenta Druydum*) was still, when he died in 1697, in manuscript ... and has remained so ever since, in the Bodleian Library at Oxford. But from the beginning it was not unknown. Parts of it were used in a new edition of Camden in 1695, and the manuscript was copied.

Anthony Wood's portrait of Aubrey is not kind, especially as Aubrey had greatly helped his Oxford fellow-antiquarian and historian. 'He was a shiftless person, roving and magotie-headed, and sometimes little better than crazed.' One adjective there does not mean quite what a modern reader may think: in the seventeenth century a maggot was a whim, a crotchet. Aubrey was certainly shiftless in personal matters, but most of his whims were those of an intelligent curiosity and he was no fool. He nails Inigo Jones's Roman theory – and an age-old fault of all theorists – very neatly in his introduction. 'But, having compared his Scheme with the Monument itself, I found he had not dealt fairly: but had made a Lesbian rule [an old mason's instrument, made of lead, for taking stone mouldings], which is conformed to the stone: that is, he framed the Monument to his own Hypothesis, which is much differing from the Thing itself.' His dissatisfaction with Jones led him to undertake his own surveying, measuring and research. Among the things he noted was the vital ring of holes now named after him. It was not until 1921 that their true importance was realized.

Later in the introduction, he reveals his own theory.

> There have been several Books writt by learned men concerning Stonehenge, much differing from one another ... Now I come in the Rear of all by comparative Arguments, to give clear evidence that these Monuments were Pagan Temples: which was not made out before, and also (with humble submission to better judgement offered) a *probability*, that they were *Temples* of the *Druids* ... This Inquiry I must confess is a gropeing in the Dark: but although I have not brought it into a clear light; I can affirm, that I have brought it from an utter darkness to a thin Mist: and I have gone farther in this Essay than any before me ...

John Aubrey

Further indeed, for this particular (and in fact cautiously stated) 'maggot' of Aubrey's about Stonehenge and Avebury being Druid temples was to dominate the scholarly and public view of the monuments for the next two centuries. That his choice fell on the Druids was not in the least a personal quirk, but almost inevitable in cultural terms. Interest in them mounted throughout the period of his life, and Celtic scholarship went back at least as far as Humphrey Llwyd, who died in 1563 (one of his works was 'Concerning Anglesey, the Island of the Druids'). The endless new discoveries in Elizabethan and Jacobean times about more primitive mankind in Africa and America had set many Englishmen wondering about their own remote ancestors. In general they remained too much under the influence of the classical historians to reject the Roman view of the North European barbarians. But the Romans had been heathens, just as seventeenth-century Rome was Anti-Christ in the flesh; and there was another increasingly studied source for the past, the Bible. It was to be the Celtic priests, the Druids, who enabled the patriot scholars to begin the debarbarization of early Britain. Their supposed simplicity, wisdom and gravity was in any case very sympathetic to contemporary religious taste in the Cromwellian age and after. As early as 1655 the two notions of 'Druids' and 'patriarchs' had been associated, and the first attempts to picture the Druids were transparently based on the popular image of the Old Testament prophets. Aylett Sammes' stern sage of 1676, with his staff, his holy book, his snowy beard, might just as well be Moses.

Though Aubrey himself nowhere takes such a romantic view of the early Britons or their priests, they fascinated him and his contemporaries deeply. We know this because he wrote for help to countless other antiquaries and men of letters all over Britain; and whether it is his Welsh cousin, the poet Henry Vaughan, on the folklore of the bardic tradition, or a true scholar like the Scot James Garden on the Picts, or Sir Thomas Browne urging him to proceed (in a letter of 1672) with his 'observations concerning the Druids', the impression is the same. To the inquiring minds of that era the mysteries of the past were as exciting a challenge as the mysteries of outer space to us today, and something had to be found to fill the blank. Aubrey tracks down references to the Druids with all the doggedness of a true literary detective, and the *Monumenta Britannica* is essentially a huge collection of clues assembled to solve a desperately difficult case. He is a delightfully paradoxical man. Superstition fascinated him, yet – at least in the *Monumenta* – he astutely derides it wherever a more rational explanation is available. He is firm that Stonehenge 'was built long time before the Romans ever knew Britaine'; he dismisses – and in this remains in advance of many twentieth-century minds – the idea of an Altar Stone, and suggests what we know is the truth: that it is simply a fallen upright. He has no time for Camden's 'artificial stone' theory, held by many scholars well into the eighteenth century, and once again is the first to demystify the legend about the method of transport. He says firmly the sarsens were dragged from the Marlborough Downs by means of timber rollers. He noted the bluestones and their weathering characteristics, as I have already mentioned. Aubrey's great virtue is in fact a rare one – a love of human imagination tempered by a love of reason. He was something more than what he is now best remembered as: the engaging tattler of the *Brief Lives*. His own self-judgment is best: 'My head was always working, never idle, and even travelling did glean some observations, some whereof are to be valued.'

Bishop Gibson and Edward Lhuyd, in their 1695 edition of Camden's *Britannia*, had summarized the theories to date. There were seven: Jones's Romans; Charleton's Danes; Sammes's Phoenicians; Aubrey's Druids; that it was a memorial to Ambrosius; to Boadicaea; and an idea that it was a monument to a native victory over the Northern French Belgae – a kind of Iron Age Waterloo. This last theory appears in two very odd pseudonymous essays written about 1670, but not printed until 1725.

Aubrey knew them well and found out that behind 'Philantiquarius Britannicus' stood a Mr Jay, of Nettlecombe, near Watchet, in Somerset; of whom nothing else is known, except that he died about 1675. Their printer, or editor, was another remarkable man, a super-polymath in this age of polymaths, Thomas Hearne, and they are to be found in his edition of Robert Mannyng's version of Peter Langtoft's chronicle, from which I have already quoted. Hearne was later satirized by Pope in the *Dunciad* as Wormius, the apotheosis of the bookworm; and his books show why. They are gigantic chains of red herrings, vast portmanteaux bursting with omnivorous knowledge, festooned with enormous notes and appendices; and delicious or maddening, according to taste ... delicious to my own. His *Langtoft* must, I suspect, have been known to T.S. Eliot, since among the other endless divagations is some very precious material on Little Gidding.

Hearne is a good example of the fascination that Stonehenge had begun to exert on scholars of his time. Reading between his many lines on the subject, one can see that the fascination lay very largely in the ambiguity. He himself held a modified Jonesian theory, of British building under Roman supervision; but above all he clearly relishes the vagueness of the evidence ... the vast Wiltshire plain that Stonehenge opened for speculation. I think it is in Hearne that one can best sense the mushrooming – since 1655 – intellectual fascination with the place; as also the dawn of a national pride in it, in its Britishness.

All these early questioners of the Wiltshire Sphinx were slightly embarrassed by its aesthetic crudity ('that Stupendious Mole', 'this rude Gigantick Pile') in terms of their own classical and baroque notions of high art; but already one can sense a chauvinism creeping in, just as it was creeping – for I am talking now of the time of Marlborough, of the beginning of Roast Beef and Old England, of the dawn of the fierce patriotism and xenophobia of the mature eighteenth century – into the country at large. The second of Jay's 1670 essays that Hearne printed as appendices, *A Fool's Bolt Soon Shott At Stonage*, already shows this. It begins very revealingly.

A Wander witt of Wiltshire, rambling to Rome to gaze at Antiquities, and there skrewing himself into the company of Antiquaries, they entreated him to illustrate unto them, that famous Monument in his Country, called *Stonage*. His Answer was, that he had never seen, scarce ever heard of, it. Whereupon, they kicked him out of doors, and bad him goe home, and see *Stonage*; and I wish all such Aesopicall Cocks, as slight these admired Stones, and other domestick Monuments ... and scrape for barley Cornes of vanity out of forreigne dunghills, might be handled, or rather footed, as he was.

Patriots, take heart. But the author goes on:

If I had been in his place, I should have been apt to have told them, that, surely, it was some heathenish temple demolished by the immediate hand of God, as an intolerable abomination unto him; yet reserving so much of it standing, as may declare what the whole was, and how, and why, so destroyed ... that we should remember that these forlorne Pillers of Stone are left to be our remembrancers, dissuading us from looking back in our hearts upon any thing of Idolatry, and persuading us ... so to describe and deride it in its uglie Coullers [colours], that none of us, or our Posterity, may returne, with Doggs, to such Vomit, or Sows to wallowing in such mire.

From that splendid piece of English bile, the writer proceeds to say that since everyone who has written on the subject confutes everyone else, since 'Pedlers and Tinckers, vamping on London way near it, may, and do, freely spend their mouthes on it', he does not see why he should not 'shoot his bolt' also on the matter.

There is nothing else in all the now enormous Stonehenge literature that can compare with this rancorous and sarcastic start to *A Fool's Bolt*. A little later, just in case any reader might think they were dealing with a mere wit, not a scholar, Jay flashes out a long list of early English historians, from Gildas and Bede on, and points out that they were all silent before Stonehenge. 'This Stonage did astonish them, and did amaze them, that they durst not labour, lest they should lose their labour, and themselves also. And if the grand Seniors, which lived so near it, above a thousand years since, could not, how shall we sillie freshmen unlock this Closet?' He then (falling through those ever-luring stone 'doors') announces that he has 'stumbled on 2 picklocks, which, if dexterously handled, will set it wide open to the world'.

They do not, of course; but the author is adamant that Stonehenge is an ancient British monument. The worthy Inigo Jones is curtly dismissed as 'Out-I-goe' Jones. Jay points out the very name is British – '*Stone hanging place*, because some remaines of it are like gallowes.' Etymology is indeed his forte, and in places it is carried to such hair-raising lengths that one half suspects that the whole essay (like his companion piece, *Claudius Caesar's Treasure*) is a seventeenth-century spoof – a dazzlingly prolonged mockery of scholarship that takes itself too seriously. But some of his ideas are shrewd, and plainly influenced Aubrey. Jay guessed that Stonehenge belonged to an original native population, before the Belgae, the Iron Age Celts from across the Channel; he concedes the Romans might have helped build it, but points out that the Greeks had contacts with ancient Britain long before Julius Caesar's time. Unfortunately he then plumps for a race of Somerset giants as builders, and cites evidence of their remains (which we can see were in fact animal fossils – one found very near Stonehenge was nearly fourteen feet long, with a tooth 'the quantity of a great wallnut'). Nothing in this bizarre piece is more striking than the domination of word over fact, of book-learned conjecture over observation. It must remain the favourite text of all amateur fools, like myself, who shoot bolts at Stonehenge.

But the major figure in the modern mythology of Stonehenge descends straight from Aubrey. William Stukeley, who was born in 1687, spent much of his life, especially his

William Stukeley

younger life, on antiquarian travels – partly as a cure for gout. A friend of Newton and a Fellow of the Royal Society, he helped found the Society of Antiquaries in 1718. His early bent was towards botany and anatomy, and he became a doctor of medicine in 1720 – and very typically, in the same year, a freemason, because he thought masonic ritual 'the remains of the mysteries of the ancients'. Already by 1726 he had built 'a temple of the Druids' in his Lincolnshire garden, next to an apple-tree with mistletoe. In 1729 he was ordained into the Church of England, though he was never a conventional clergyman. Warburton called him a mixture of 'simplicity, drollery, absurdity, ingenuity, superstition and antiquarianism'. In another of his books in 1736 he tried to demonstrate that all heathen mythology was derived from sacred history, and that (of all pagan gods) Bacchus, the god of wine, was really Jehovah. The 'drollery' is also well proven. Two years before he died in 1765 he had to wear spectacles for the first time in his church. He preached on the evils of too much study, from the text 'Now we see through a glass darkly'. A year later he postponed matins for an hour so that his congregation could go out and watch an eclipse.

Some aspects of his quite definitely crazed character remind one of 'maggoty-headed' Aubrey, and it is fitting that the major obsession of his life seems to have come from a reading of a copy of Aubrey's manuscript in 1718. From then on, ignoring all Aubrey's qualifications, such as his maintaining that the monument must be pre-Christian, Stukeley was blindingly, and blindly, certain that the Druids were the priests of one of the lost tribes of Israel, descended from Abraham to the Phoenician Hercules, and had come here from the Near East, bringing the purest form of primitive Christianity and 'the notion and expectation of the Messiah' (together with 'knowledge of the magnetical compass') aboard their ships. They also obligingly showed remarkable premonitory taste in terms of eighteenth-century church politics, since Stukeley assures us that they enshrined 'the regular and golden chain of religion . . . which keeps the medium between slovenly fanaticism and popish pageantry'. They were safe Church of England men, in short, and not to be held responsible for the future horrors of Calvin and Rome.

All this was given to the world in his two books, on Stonehenge in 1740, on Avebury in 1743; a projected third (the over-all title was to be *Patriarchal Religion*) was never written. But the two were quite enough to launch his 'vision'. Others soon came to develop it to even more fervent extremes.

It is the Christianity that is new, not the notion of a Near Eastern origin. A version of that is to be found in Geoffrey of Monmouth, six hundred years earlier: there the Celts claim descendence from the Trojans. This seems in fact to have been a propaganda story, like the Arthurian cycle, conjured up by the Celtic bards towards the end of the Dark Ages, long after the Saxon invasion. There is no mention of it in Bede, who wrote in the early eighth century. Then Sammes had already suggested Phoenicia, and Stukeley had read in John Norden's history of Cornwall (Norden visited the county in 1584) of a miners' legend there concerning the 'attle sarrazin', the Saracens' rubbish, or ancient mineworkings. Some extraordinary folk-memory of the early Phoenician and Greek exploitation of Cornish tin and lead had somehow survived to Elizabethan times. There were in any case many classical texts, from Herodotus on, about this pre-Roman contact between the Mediterranean and Britain.

All this side of his theory is not implausible, indeed not too far removed from the diffusion theory of very recent times; and of course no evidence was then known for North European cultures earlier than the Celtic – no one suspected that societies without written record might have existed. Nor was all of Stukeley's head in the mystical clouds. For a start his travels had given him a far greater comparative knowledge of ancient British sites than any of his contemporaries; and however fantastic his deductions he remained a sharp and accurate observer. Though the observatory theories of Stonehenge are usually dated to John Smith's *Choir Gaur, The Grand Orrery of the Ancient Druids* of 1771, Stukeley had already noted 'a greater exactness in placing with regard to the quarters of the heavens than one would expect' in his sites.

Stukeley's general method was, as he said himself, 'a diffusive one, not pretending to a formal and stiff scholastic proof'. One ugly little lack of 'stiff scholastic proof' concerns Aubrey; not once did Stukeley acknowledge his huge debt in that direction – mainly, one suspects, because he knew what Aubrey's much more sceptical mind would have made of this cloud city built on his own cautious foundations. This in itself is tell-tale of a general phenomenon, for English scholarship went into a decline for several decades from about the 1730s on: that is, it became rather too susceptible to general social climate and tended increasingly to fall, as Stukeley himself conspicuously did, between two stools – in his case, that of the scholar and that of the reverend mystic. One attraction of his theory to the general reader of his time was also that once and for all it excused the 'barbarousness' of Stonehenge in aesthetic terms ... for what did that matter before Christianity revealed in its simplest, noblest, most ancient form? It also neatly suggested that the British were, in effect, a chosen people.

Stukeley's general mistrust of the spirit of scepticism was of course paralleled in the growth of religious dissent – the impatience with the dormant Church of England of the Early Georgian period. The evangelist John Wesley held his first field meetings near Bristol in 1739, the year before Stukeley's book appeared. The century began quarrelling very early with its own seeming appearance and drift. Outwardly it might grow more formal, more rational, more classical and Augustan, but the great counter-movement – the search for more feeling,

An engraving by William Stukeley, 1724

more simplicity, more morality, all that was to swell into the Romantic Movement and its accompanying political revolutions – had already germinated by the 1740s. What made Stukeley so persuasive was less his argument than his epoch.

Archaeologically the Celts of the La Tène culture, whose shaman-priests we call Druids (Old Celtic for 'magician'), can have had nothing at all to do with the building of Stonehenge. They did not arrive in any numbers in Britain (which owes its name to them) until at least a thousand years after the final building phase of about 1500 B.C. Yet some of their own religious beliefs may very well have been formed by much earlier ones. Stukeley did his best to give them a whiter-than-white image; but there is a good deal of evidence that the early Celtic was not one of the most endearing cultures the world has known. Despite the current neo-Stukeleian passion for it, half-based on mysticism, half on racial chauvinism, any dispassionate reader – and even allowing for the fact that all the contemporary accounts are written by Roman enemies – must find it distinctly savage. The Celts were the Red Indians of ancient Europe, and like the Red Indians, they cannot be quite let off on the grounds of foreign exploitation; we can admire their fierce resistance to the Romans rather more easily than some of the values they were protecting. It must be added that they seem to have shared something of the Red Indian genius for living in psychological harmony with nature; and no novelist can do anything but fall to his or her knees before another of their gifts. The Celts are among the finest story-tellers and myth-makers of all human history.

'Celtic' is more a linguistic or cultural description than a racial one. Their origin lies in the Indo-European world, and parallels can be found with the ancient peoples of the other India, beyond Aden. They were horse-worshippers – never a happy augury, then or now; they practised a form of suttee, relatives and servants being burnt with their dead chieftains. They were also devoted scalpers or head-hunters, very much of that breed (and endless menace to other humanity) who believe nothing more glorious – better dead than Roman – than leaving this world in battle.

They seem originally to have had three classes of priests, Vates or augurs, Bards or tribal celebrators, and the Druids, responsible for religious ritual, medicine and the law; but all these functions became subsumed in the end in the Druids. One of their methods of augury was to kill a victim by sword or axe from behind, and to see how he fell. Druid teaching – another echo from India – was all oral and done very much on a guru-pupil basis, and it took many years to become proficient. The ambitious went to Britain to finish their studies. Caesar records a strong interest in astronomy; and that their calendar was based on lunar months, while they counted passage of time in nights, not days. There is another mention of their holding great festivals at nineteen-year intervals, which must immediately remind us of the long moon cycle that the first Stonehenge may have been built to detect. What they actually made of Stonehenge and the other European megalithic monuments we shall never know; perhaps they felt towards them as we do towards the Easter Island statues today, largely at a loss. But it seems more likely they were not entirely unaware of their past function and significance.

Early Celtic religion was very much a polytheistic one, a matter of countless sacred places and animals; they had an especial veneration for water, remembrance of which runs in the still Celtic names of many European and British rivers and the countless 'holy' wells. Their two principal deities seem to have been a triadic mother-goddess – white virgin, red wife, black crone, as in Minoan Crete and ancient Greece – and a warrior sun-god (corresponding to Apollo) called Lugh. Lyons in France, Leyden in Holland and many other places still bear his name, and the most famous Celt of our own era, King Arthur, is essentially an epiphany of him.

The mother-goddess and the sun-god do not suggest any great discontinuity from the past, or no more than there is forward with the arrival of Christ and the Virgin Mary, but all the Roman writers bear witness to the fact that the Druids' holy places were usually in caves or groves. In A.D. 61, on a punitive expedition in Anglesey in North Wales, the Romans took good care to destroy all these sacred-grove temples that they could find. It may seem not unreasonable to infer that Stonehenge cannot in fact have been of any great significance in the true Druid period, or the Romans would not have left it standing. On-site evidence for Celtic religious use is inconclusive. Iron Age pottery has been found, and there are graves and barrows in the area; but nothing suggests the importance of previous times, though there is one small hint that the monument was still respected. The land around it was left untouched by Iron Age farmers.

This in fact raises one last mystery about Stonehenge, which I hinted at earlier. It might in Sherlock Holmes's terms be called 'The Peculiar Case of the Fallen Stones'. The truth is that more has fallen or vanished into thin air than one would expect in the natural course of events and in view of the superbly sound construction methods. One sarsen upright was badly damaged at the base when it was being erected, and had to be wedged up to reach its proper height; but even this comparative 'bodge' did not begin to tilt until nearly four thousand years later. The stones are also far deeper set than anywhere else in prehistoric Britain. Even more striking, as any air photograph shows, is the very odd distribution of fallen and still standing stones. It is overwhelmingly the westward semi-circle that has suffered. Another ominous clue lies underground, where there is a massive distribution of sarsen and bluestone chips that cannot be explained simply as masons' debris.

In short, it looks singularly as if someone did at some point try to raze Stonehenge to the ground. In naming the culprits Professor Atkinson will not choose between the Romans and medieval peasants. Against the Romans is the fact that in one area the quantity of Roman pottery finds tallies suspiciously well with that of the stone chips. We also know that with the British Celts they abandoned their more usual policy of adapting foreign cult-buildings to their own religion and went in much more for a scorched-earth *régime*. Yet it is difficult to imagine they lacked the authority, thoroughness and engineering skills to do a full demolition; and there is well-documented evidence not far away that the medieval church, or *its* policy, should quite definitely go in the dock. A very great destruction of the sarsens took place at Avebury in the early fourteenth century, probably inspired by the witch-mania of the period. In many cases it was not considered enough merely to tumble the heathen stones. They were buried out of sight and touch beneath the ground. Perhaps at Stonehenge it was found more expedient or easier to smash some or parts of them to smithereens – to break the magic circle, rather than obliterate it completely.

Other things we know about Celtic religion do indicate a general continuity of belief, even if the nature of the cult-places changed. There is the very special reverence in which they held the oak and the mistletoe, especially when they occurred (as they rarely do in Britain) in conjunction. Quite apart from the fact that oak-worship is almost universal in the ancient world, Neolithic builders seem to have favoured it in their wood henges, and the oak grew abundantly in prehistoric times in the Stonehenge area. Even better evidence has been found in some very early graves, contemporary with Stonehenge, in the Scilly Isles off Cornwall. Funerary ashes there are of oak; but the oak does not grow on the islands, and must have been imported for religious reasons. Many superstitions emphasize the tree's protective and benign qualities, as with 'gospel' and 'marriage' oaks. It had powers against lightning; acorn buttons at the end of things like blind-cords are not there just for ornament. Nor, if one had to choose a plant to symbolize the full moon, could one do much better than the mistletoe; which is never found at ground level, whose appearance and disappearance is always capricious, whose round white berries appear at mid-winter, when all else is dead.

Finally, there is that haunting central motif of so many of the greatest Celtic legends: the trio of trusting king, torn queen, adulterous knight. Because almost all our versions come from feudal times, we tend to see it as a vehicle for the conflict between sexual passion and social duty, between faith and treachery, Christian guilt and pagan innocence, and all the rest. But it also has curious echoes of a widespread feature of primitive fertility religion: the real or symbolic mating of a potent young man and a female representative of the earth-goddess, sometimes associated with the subsequent ritual sacrifice of one or both. Here the king stands for the secular or priestly power that maintains due observance, and picks a surrogate or scapegoat for both the 'marriage' and the sacrifice; the queen stands for the promise of fertility invoked; and the knight is at the same time the victim and the saviour of his society.

Gorlois, Ygraine, Uther Pendragon; Arthur, Guinevere, Lancelot; Mark, Isolde, Tristan ... these and many other eternal – and eternally popular – Celtic triangles may seem remote from Neolithic and Bronze Age Stonehenge. It is quite possible that nowhere is the Druid connection closer.

But nothing now can ever restore Stonehenge to the Druids archaeologically. Once again we are faced with a totally false hypothesis, a huge construct based on nothing, and in this case one that in its essence is far from dead in the public mind. The Druid theory may be scientifically worthless, but the essentially mystical approach to the place remains very alive. It attracts present-day 'worshippers' for exactly the same reason that it attracted book-worms like Thomas Hearne two and a half centuries ago. The very – and quite proper – caution of modern scientists in their conclusions about the ancient realities of Stonehenge effectively leaves a huge empty space, a field for speculation, in the less scientific mind. In this Stonehenge remains almost like a blank sheet of paper – in a world where, in terms of knowledge, blank sheets become increasingly rare things.

We know from not too dissimilar phenomena, like the Yeti, the Loch Ness Monster, the Bermuda Triangle, the U.F.O. 'sightings', that something in the human mind craves these blank spaces, and theories about them, however nonsensical, however rationally and statistic-ally improbable; which is in part, of course, because they can never be quite totally disproved. That the Loch Ness Monster so resolutely avoids all publicity is not a strict proof that it does not exist; nor is the absence of any observable magical powers at Stonehenge of any significance to its present votaries. There is always a retreat into the last cloud of unknowing: that you must believe before you will be allowed to feel or see.

To treat Stonehenge, or for that matter God, with a quasi-religious awe is tautological; what is really being treated with religious awe is simply religious awe, and that is the proper thing to judge, not the folly or wisdom of its being especially attached to a few curious stones in Wiltshire, or an old man's face.

Certainly in artistic terms – and most of the early explanations of Stonehenge belong much more now in the realm of art than that of science – my contention that most human progress arises by accident, and very often in the course of trying to prove hypotheses formed on basic false premises, holds good. English art would be infinitely the poorer without Stukeley's great lunge into the historically absurd. Every period needs myths, or scientifically unprov-able explanations of reality, that it can use to express itself. Their intrinsic value is far less important than the richness of the reaction they provoke.

Long before 1700 an astute oriental visitor – that favourite mask of social critics of the time – to Britain might have noted a dangerous and growing schism between human behaviour and human knowledge: between actual and rational social institution, between established and intelligent religion, between what was and what ought to be. We think of the rise of eighteenth-century sensibility, which for all its later excesses and narcissisms was fundamentally an awakening of conscience through sympathy and empathy, as something 'new'. But all sensibility (not least our own present concern for ecological sanity) is partially backward, seeking of a return to the past, which is why it can so often seem childish and why it is so often a sitting duck for the cynic. The intellect is always for greater complexity, increased distance, irony, objectivity, futurity; all its energies are essentially games-playing ones, to do with testing, solving, outmanœuvring, finally winning. The energy of feeling is poured into closing gaps, into shortcutting intellectual process, into faith in ideals of personal behaviour and public institution – whence its frequent discontentedness. It is also, both in its perceptions and its hopes, intensely immediate. Feeling is now, and wants change now, not in some logically planned or vaguely promised future.

The seventeenth century saw the birth of all our natural sciences and had by its end harvested, in terms of the past, an astounding crop of new knowledge; yet which remained, so to speak, still locked away in a barn ... unmilled and inedible, unimpinging on actual society. But increased sensibility is not just a blind reaction to scientific discovery and greater understanding of empirical method, the recalcitrant heart trying to slow the mind down; it is also a logical and inevitable consequence of it. If Bacon and the new method demanded an end to scholasticism, to theory based on traditional authority and book-knowledge, and erected experiment and direct observation as the twin gods of a wise humanity, feeling could only follow ... and experiment itself with direct observation and its emotional consequences. We have only to look at our own century's closed fascist societies to see the lethal connection between censorship of information and death of fellow-feeling. At its best, sensibility is objective knowledge – whether emitted by science, state or church – translated, or digested, into human terms. The apple falls, in Eden as in Newton's orchard; and always the greater knowledge the falling brings must also in the end provoke greater feeling. There is no more fixed and inalienable law in human psychology.

Stukeley's Druids and their primitive purity were to colour the most vital and history-changing aspect of his century: the movement of Dissent. As Stukeley rode and rode during the first three decades of the century in search of lost ruins, so a little later were men like the Wesleys and Whitehead to ride in their own evangelical pursuit of ruined souls and lost religious sentiment. John Wesley's incomparable power as preacher seems to have derived not from any particular oratorical skill but from the intense conviction he managed to put behind, or in, his habitually quiet voice; and something of the same is true of Stukeley. In retrospect we can see that Dissent in its broadest sense, this quality of conviction in non-conformity, played a far more important part in political than in religious history. Religion was simply a vehicle for a much deeper sea-change in human self-consciousness. In its narrower sense, Dissent might outwardly seem concerned only for freedom of sectarian belief. But its effect was to speak for all individual and social liberty of conscience, or feeling, and went far beyond mere religious form.

Of course it was not at that time sufficient to argue this on abstract grounds; it needed to be derived from authority. The Dissenters went to the Bible, the more sceptical to the notion of the Noble Savage, where once again Stukeley can be counted as a progenitor. The idea that things will be better in the future is mankind's greatest illusion; but the idea that they were once better in the past runs a very close second. 'Contemporary civilization is corruption' is the real message lying behind *Stonehenge Restor'd to the British Druids*. In spite of its inherent conservatism, the counter-image of the noble primitive did provide an opposition to the growing national chauvinisms of the period ... and, in Rousseau's hands, did far more than that. Whatever the archaeological foolishness of the Druid theory, whatever its patriarchal narrowness in religious terms, its effect was essentially humanist.

It helped the eighteenth century question itself in the way it most deeply needed to; and our general debt to it lies in an area that has nothing to do with science, but with the way we feel both past and present. The astonishingly long run the theory had can indeed be seen as a triumph of unconscious feeling over scientific common-sense. A number of Stukeley's learned contemporaries, such as Benjamin Martin ('That this Temple was certainly built by the Druids ... is far from being a point clearly and fairly proved'), did not in fact like Stukeley's theories at all and argued against them; yet how much the poorer we should all have been if those cleverer scholars had been successful, and killed the idea at the outset.

BLAKE'S BOLT

OUR LAST DEBT to Stukeley is more personal. He signally helped a far greater human being pose some even more challenging questions, and ones we have still not answered. William Blake seized on the Druids to embody a much deeper fault in humanity than religious sloth or libertine scepticism. References to them run like a sinister musical *motif* all through his prophetic books.

> ... I have Murdered Albion! Ah!
> In Stone-henge & on London Stone & in the Oak Groves of Malden
> I have Slain him in my Sleep with the knife of the Druid.

So cried England-Britannia in *Jerusalem*, when she wakes on the cold body of Albion, or primal nature. The Druids stood archetypally in Blake's mind for that abomination, Priesthood. In *The Marriage of Heaven and Hell* he tells how Priesthood arises. In the beginning the ancient poets 'animated all sensible objects with Gods or Geniuses.'

> Till a system was formed, which some took advantage of, & enslav'd the vulgar by attempting to realize or abstract the mental deities from their objects: thus began Priesthood;
> Choosing forms of worship from poetic tales.
> And at length they pronounc'd that the Gods had order'd such things.
> Thus men forgot that All deities reside in the human breast.

Till a system was formed ... Blake's profound and magnificent hatred of this tendency in man to imprison himself, to build walls of ritual and tradition, theory and creed, around his soul, still has something to tell us about Stonehenge. We may today think it rather ludicrously unjust to the Stonehenge builders to see nothing in their monument but a first step into intellectual and spiritual slavery.

Where the Druids rear'd their Rocky Circles to make permanent Remembrance
Of Sin, & the Tree of Good and Evil sprang from the Rocky Circle & Snake
Of the Druid ...

Yet we *are* dealing with an early technological masterpiece, both in its building and its
function; we *do* now know only too well the cost of technology in terms of our bodies, our
minds and our souls; and science *is* a system, and a particularly jealous one in regard to
other systems. No Stukeley, no eccentric but fertile visionary, stands much chance today;
what visionaries we have had recently, the Velikovskys and the Von Dänikens, can try only
to beat science at its own game, and fail almost before they begin. That science is the dominant system in terms of what now goes on at the site, as it is over so much of the rest of
our lives, is inevitable; and only a fool would argue that this should not be so in terms of
conservation and excavation. But the danger comes when it attempts to dictate our personal
experience and perception of the whole, for this is the essence of what Blake feared in Druidism: not just knowing for oneself, but knowing for everybody else as well.

More and more Western society threatens to forget that other systems of perceiving,
understanding and deriving benefit from external reality exist. More and more we are forced
to join an extreme; either pure science or lunatic fringe, in neither of which can lie the answer.
Not in the first, because it has to exclude the reality of individual mentality and feeling.
Not in the second, because it will base itself on nothing else. More and more all external
objects become druidized – in the modern jargon, reified. A natural phenomenon – even,
God save us, an artistic one – is reduced to the number of hard facts to be extracted from
it. It is what Blake means in the passage I have just quoted. When he speaks of the priests
(the masters of any system) who enslaved the ordinary people 'by attempting to realize ...
the mental deities' he is using 'realize' in a very literal sense: to make external objects of
the mental deities, to take them out of the mind and turn them into idols. Science is the
most formidable of the idols that man has ever realized, in this literal sense.

I am not pleading for Stonehenge to be reconverted to a 'cathedral' for contemporary
mystics. Most of them badly need a course in Blake, or true mysticism, which always passes
far beyond a voguish reverence for idols and ikons and gurus, and infinitely beyond a hermetic
love of the mysterious for its own sake. Nor is true mysticism ever about a return to the
impossible. I repeat, mystical feelings about Stonehenge are feelings about mystical feeling;
and the greater their attachment to the one place, indeed to anything but humanity itself,
the more we should be suspicious of their value and their honesty. The true mystic may
have external and local preferences, as Blake himself markedly did, in the symbolic expression
of the inner truth; but that sort of truth has no truck with good and bad vibes, energy centres,

place healing and all the rest of the debased coinage of so much contemporary 'esoteric knowledge'. Such egotistic credulity is only a hair's-breadth removed from drinking powdered Stonehenge as medicine.

Yet my true and perhaps rather paradoxical point is that even at its mindless worst, such an attitude betrays something valuable not in, but of our age. It cannot be coincidence that the corner of this globe where instant mysticism is most in fashion is also the most mechanized and gadget-filled, the greatest slave of applied science. I asked a Californian once why it was so, and her answer was brief: 'Too much.' One superfluity we all suffer from is that of trivial knowledge, of useless facts. Useless knowledge diminishes man. All knowledge kills possibility, which is excellent for science, but far less beneficial to the individual. Choosing not to know, in an increasingly 'known', structured, ordained, predictable world, becomes almost a freedom, a last refuge of the self. It is not that we cannot see the wood for the trees; we can hardly even see the trees themselves now through all the fact-cloud of botanies, taxonomies, biochemistries – the sheer quantity of knowledge we have of them as *things*. Such knowledge is essential for the professional forester; what is not essential is that we should all behave like professional foresters, or tolerate their expecting us to.

The attraction of Stonehenge here is very simple: there are not yet enough facts about it to bury it in certainty, in a scientific final solution to all its questions. Its great *present* virtue is precisely that something so concrete, so *sui generis*, so individualized, should still evoke so much imprecision of feeling and thought. This is in fact a criterion we habitually apply to the greatest works of art. We say of them that they are inexhaustible, that every age has to interpret them anew, and so on; and what we tend to forget is that lunatic fringes and false mysticism are cheap prices to pay for the existence of such phenomena. They are certainly cheaper than the alternative, which is to treat all artefacts, from Stonehenge to a Bach fugue, as properly apprehensible only through science, or conscious knowing.

But even on science's own terms, digging pits and trenches is not the only archaeology. There is another whose field is the human imagination, and Stonehenge is as important a site for this as it is for archaeology proper; and as with archaeology proper, all its relics and manifestations are valid. They are not invalid, and so discardable, because they do not add to our strictly scientific knowledge of the monument or can be proven wrong by it. That Blake swallowed Stukeley's theory almost whole has nothing whatever to do with the uses he put it to or the deeper truths he found behind it; to claim it does only strengthens his vision of the evil and danger in all reifying and self-imprisoning systems. Of course any expression of the imagination can be valued both scientifically and artistically; but as evidence of the human mind, ancient or modern, each is good. We have no more right to consign what Stonehenge has provoked – and still provokes – in the individual imagination to oblivion (or the lunatic fringe) than we have to bulldoze the place to the ground because we now have better observatories and know far more about architectural design and handling large masonry.

The other Stonehenge, this vast labyrinth of words, pictures, speculations, feelings, impressions, may never be quite so important as the scientists' Stonehenge, but it is no less real in any deep or sane sense of human history. Almost everyone who visits the monument feels this, though in a negative way. It is a common-place that the actual physical presence is, to most first visitors, much smaller than they expected. This double reality is similarly betrayed in almost every artistic representation of the monument, from the sixteenth century on. Never can a building have had its actual scale and height *vis-à-vis* man so persistently exaggerated or its surroundings so romanticized, both before and after the Romantic Movement proper. It is not that artists, or ordinary visitors, want Stonehenge to be larger than it is. It is larger than it is.

Stonehenge has done sterling service in aid of the imagination, and I think it is time the native imagination did a little more to repay the debt than offering it mere physical protection. The old pastoral setting of before this century, of Aubrey's 'Downes stockt with numerous Flocks of Sheeps, the Turfe rich & fragrant with Thyme & Burnet', of the happenstance stones in the upland steppe peopled only by nut-brown shepherdesses, is gone for ever and cannot return. Today is crowds, cars, coaches, lavatories, shops, unconsciously reified people trailing round consciously reified things. All skeleton, no heart. We can never regain the old landscape or the emotional effect of the old monument, just as a wild animal in a zoo can never affectively resemble the wild animal in its natural habitat. Only a very few now, the fortunate archaeologist, the fortunate photographer, can hope to have a glimpse of it. The rest of us must stay as imprisoned, as rejected, as the stones themselves; and like them, can only stand and wait for better days.

Perhaps Blake was right, and if we must point to one place where Adam and Eve definitively left the Garden of Eden, it is on this Wiltshire hill; which may be why something in all of us has always felt a secret humility there, a mortality, the presence of a brooding enigma beyond all our formulations of it ... to do with a step that can never be retraced, but whose wisdom we can still doubt – and must doubt, if we are to survive. The one Stonehenge is made incomplete by the ravages of time; the other, because something in it has yet to be finished.

But now my own bolt falls, and the last word on this strange, this immemorial mirror of *Homo faber*, man the maker, shall go to a poet; a lesser than Blake, but a kinder, Siegfried Sassoon.

What is Stonehenge? It is the roofless past;
Man's ruinous myth; his uninterred adoring
Of the unknown in sunrise cold and red;
His quest of stars that arch his doomed exploring.

And what is Time but shadows that were cast
By these storm-sculptured stones while centuries fled?
The stones remain; their stillness can outlast
The skies of history hurrying overhead.

From Blake's *Jerusalem*

Acknowledgments

I must thank Mr Rodney Legg of the Dorset Publishing Company for allowing me to consult proofs of his forthcoming facsimile – and first – edition of John Aubrey's *Monumenta Britannica*, an event that he will forgive me for saying comes nearly three centuries after it was due; Dr Barbara Eastman, Mr T.R. Gilbert and Mr Laurence Whistler, for respectively drawing my attention to the English journal of Lodewijck Huygens, Benjamin Martin's account of Stonehenge and Siegfried Sassoon's poem in *The Heart's Journey*. I should also like to thank the librarians of the Wiltshire Archaeological and Natural History Society at Devizes for their kindness to an unannounced stranger. Of the many books I have read I must cite two that have been especially helpful. One is Aubrey Burl's *Prehistoric Avebury* (Yale University Press, 1979). The other is the bible of all modern students of the monument, R.J.C. Atkinson's *Stonehenge* (Pelican revised edition, 1979). Since I am in my introduction perhaps not quite the soul of kindness to Professor Atkinson, at least let me here pay sincere homage to the scrupulous scholarship enshrined in his indispensable book.

John Fowles

I would like to acknowledge the following people, each of whom has made a significant contribution to this book. Larry Keenan, Larry Reif, Thomas F. Woodhouse, Jim Silberman, Hank Kranzler, Tom Meyer, Ursula Gropper, Tom Maschler, Ian Craig, Nikon Professional Services, Arthur Shartsis, John Poppy. Readers may like to know that the equipment I used to take the photographs for this book was Nikon Nikkormat E.L. and F.E. 35 mm camera bodies, with lenses ranging from 20 mm to 200 mm.

Barry Brukoff

The publishers would like to thank the following for permission to reproduce pictures: Aerofilms, p. 47; the Master and Fellows of Corpus Christi College, Cambridge, p. 88; Mary Evans Picture Library, pp. 91, 93, 105, 106; the Fotomas Index, pp. 8, 38, 42, 83, 127; the National Library of Scotland, p. 92.